2-13

D1237903

11 22
STRAND PRICE
5 00

779.99748
P

207968

NINETEENTH-CENTURY PHOTOGRAPHY IN PHILADELPHIA

250 Historic Prints from The Library Company of Philadelphia

by
KENNETH FINKEL
Curator of Prints

Published in Cooperation with
The Library Company of Philadelphia by
DOVER PUBLICATIONS, INC.
NEW YORK

Dedicated to the memory of
JIMMY BRENT

Frontispiece: Detail of Illustration 95.

Copyright © 1980 by The Library Company of Philadelphia.
All rights reserved under Pan American and International Copyright Conventions.

Published in Canada by General Publishing Company, Ltd., 30 Lesmill Road, Don Mills, Toronto, Ontario.
Published in the United Kingdom by Constable and Company, Ltd., 10 Orange Street, London WC2H 7EG.

Nineteenth-Century Photography in Philadelphia: 250 Historic Prints from The Library Company of Philadephia is a new work, first published by Dover Publications, Inc., in 1980 in cooperation with The Library Company of Philadelphia.

Book design by Carol Belanger Grafton

International Standard Book Number: 0-486-23932-2
Library of Congress Catalog Card Number: 79-54401

Manufactured in the United States of America
Dover Publications, Inc.
180 Varick Street
New York, N.Y. 10014

PREFACE

The Library Company of Philadelphia is America's oldest cultural institution. Founded by Benjamin Franklin in 1731, it was, for most of its 250 years, Philadelphia's major library. Any such institution that matures with its city cannot help building an impressive collection of prints and drawings; the Library Company has long served as a repository for architectural drawings, political cartoons, portraits, maps and all manner of historical iconography. Approached with scholarly enthusiasm in the latter half of this century, the entire collection of books, prints and manuscripts gradually has been recognized as a valuable asset to learning. Like other parts of the Library's holdings that were unseen for generations, the photographs too have been brought to light.

Most of the Library Company's photograph collection was already acquired, through purchase and gift, by the turn of the century. Its core is the result of the activities of two voracious mid-nineteenth-century collectors, Charles A. Poulson and John McAllister, Jr., both of whom patronized working photographers. Only within the last several years have the Library's photographic holdings been discovered to be exceptional and deserving of more attention. The assistance of the National Endowment for the Arts and the Samuel S. Fels Fund allowed the organization of the collection to begin in earnest. As this work progressed, the significance of the collection in the context of nineteenth-century Philadelphia photography became understood, and through further purchase and gift many of the important lacunae have been filled. We have many to thank for their generous gifts which have enriched the selection in this publication: Hugh P. Brinton, Francis James Dallett, Morris Finkel, Mr. and Mrs. Maro S. Hunting, Manuel Kean, Mrs. A. Douglas Oliver, Mrs. L. M. C. Smith and the Barra Foundation.

This book would be of little value were it not for the advice, inspiration and guidance of many people. I am particularly indebted to M. Elizabeth Cropper, Dale Jensen, Manuel Kean, Marie Korey, Phil Lapsansky, Lisa Lieberman, Gordon M. Marshall, Bernard F. Reilly, Jr., Linda Stanley and William Stapp. The generous assistance of James E. Mooney, Peter J. Parker and the staff of the Historical Society of Pennsylvania; Dr. Whitfield J. Bell, Jr. at the American Philosophical Society; Robert F. Looney at the Free Library of Philadelphia; Kneeland McNulty at the Philadelphia Museum of Art; Michal McMahon and Harvey Miller at the Franklin Institute; and Andrew Eskind and staff at the International Museum of Photography at George Eastman House (Rochester, N.Y.), was essential and is heartily appreciated. I would like to acknowledge the fine copy work of Joseph J. Kelly and the prints made by Thomas Landon Davies of The Photography Place from original negatives. The kind and cooperative staff of The Library Company of Philadelphia is warmly to be thanked, as is its Board of Directors. But without the energy and insight of the Librarian, Edwin Wolf 2nd, this publication would never have been. To Mr. Wolf I am especially grateful.

K. F.

NOTE: Only in the introduction and section on photographers are pictures used that are not in the collection of the Library Company. The owners are identified in the captions. Reproductions appear actual size when possible.

NOTE: Prints for reproduction of the photographs in this volume owned by The Library Company of Philadelphia are available. Requests should be addressed to The Library Company of Philadelphia, 1314 Locust Street, Philadelphia, Pennsylvania 19107.

CONTENTS

INTRODUCTION

Photography pulled at the seams of mid-nineteenth-century sensibilities. It invited manipulation of the physical world, allowing an audience to choose and possess their favorite parts. Photographs were quiet illusions that forced people to reorganize their idea of the universe. The ability to make pictures with light was a gift to civilization analogous to that of fire or writing; as in the myths of Prometheus and Hermes, it changed forever the way in which people thought. Stories of how photography came into being were told again and again, refined and compiled, for this advancement was immediately recognized as a powerful shaper of the modern mind, and its inventors were endowed with special virtues of genius.[1]

The history of photography's origins is laced with characters and motivations that make it an epic. To capture the reflection of a landscape on the ground glass of a *camera obscura* was a recurring dream for eighteenth- and nineteenth-century travelers. Success was approached in the 1830s as William Henry Fox Talbot in England, and Louis-Jacques-Mandé Daguerre with Nicéphore Niépce in France, proceeded in different ways toward a similar end. Talbot, a scholar and an aristocrat, made photochemical images on paper as early as 1835. Daguerre was the proprietor of a diorama, a showplace where the public was entertained by large historical paintings with illusionistic effects. He made unique images on silver-plated copper in 1837. Both governments recognized these achievements and the rights to profit from them. Talbot received patents; and in return for the rights to his process, France awarded Daguerre a pension for life.

In a gesture toward the progress of civilization, the French government gave Daguerre's process to the world in August 1839. Much European and American effort was expended to improve and apply the relatively simple technique. It was an open competition that included hundreds of people, mostly scientists, artists and entrepreneurs who desired knowledge, profit or recognition.

In Philadelphia, resourceful men took an immediate interest in the daguerreotype.[2] One of these was Joseph Saxton, who was responsible for the balances at the United States Mint and otherwise known for his contribution to the engineering of metals. Saxton read the Parisian accounts, made a camera from a cigar box and a magnifying glass, and produced several images from a window of the Mint building.[3] These daguerreotypes, made before October 22, 1839, were soon considered precious relics, and one was deposited at the Historical Society of Pennsylvania, where it remains today. It is the earliest surviving daguerreotype made in the United States (Fig. 1). Despite his brief impact on the history of photography in America, Saxton shares the patriarchal aura enjoyed by Talbot and Daguerre. Hardly a personality in this history, Saxton is a symbol of American genius and its ability to respond deftly when civilization advances.

Accurate or not, the myth-like anecdotes about the pioneers have been compiled and represent the history of early photography. This history is supported by dozens of superlative images. Hardly a publication appears, hardly an exhibition or auction takes place, without a few of the recognized international classics: "Sir John F. W. Herschel" by Julia Margaret Cameron, "Delacroix" by Nadar and "The Steerage" by Alfred Stieglitz. These great pictures have helped to make photography respectable but our preoccupation with makers, subjects and prices has distracted us from a fuller understanding of photographic imagery. As curators, collectors and dealers continue to sift through nineteenth-century holdings, such arbitrary and superficial values will continue to project additional photographers into favor. But we must recognize the pitfalls of taste and realize that a true understanding will not emerge in the telling of anecdotes, nor will it emerge in the marketplace. It must be a result of looking at and thinking about photographs.

In the nineteenth-century representation of the physical world there are five distinct classes of images: people, places, objects, events and views.[4] Three successive kinds of images can be distinguished within

---

[1] The inventors themselves emphasized a biographical perspective in order to establish preeminence. Nearly every successive account of photography in the nineteenth and twentieth centuries has recounted the achievements of Wedgwood, Davy, Herschel, Niépce, Daguerre and Talbot in a ritualistic introduction.

[2] M. A. Root, *The Camera and the Pencil* (Philadelphia: M. A. Root, 1864), pp. 351–352. According to Root, the earliest local experimenters with the daguerreotype in addition to Joseph Saxton were "Robert Cornelius, Drs. Paul Beck Goddard, Parker, Bird, and Kennedy, Professors John Frazer and Walter R. Johnson, William G. Mason, Dr. Wildman, and others."

[3] *United States Gazette,* October 24, 1839; Root, p. 351.

[4] In *The Pencil of Nature,* originally published 1844–46 (reprinted by Da Capo Press, N.Y., 1969), text opposite pl. III, William Henry Fox Talbot suggested the use of photography for the recording of valuable household objects. François Arago observed in his report to the Chamber of Deputies, July 6, 1839, that if such treasures as Egyptian hieroglyphics were copied when discovered, their accidental or malicious destruction would not be as severe a loss: [L.-M.-J.] Daguerre, *An Historical and Descriptive Account of the various Processes of the Daguerréotype and the Diorama,* originally published 1839 (reprinted by Winter House, Ltd., N.Y., 1971), p. 22. More recently, John Szarkowski made five categories for photographs in an exhibition at The Museum of Modern Art in New York, *The Photographer's Eye* (N.Y., 1966).

FIG. 1. "The first heliograph ever made in Philadelphia." Northeast from the United States Mint at Chestnut and Juniper Streets. Daguerreotype by Joseph Saxton, October 1839. The Historical Society of Pennsylvania.

FIG. 2. Peter S. Du Ponceau. Sixth-plate daguerreotype by Robert Cornelius, 1839.
The American Philosophical Society.

each class. Photographs made before 1845 were often experimental and always constituted the most unsophisticated impressions. In the next period, roughly 1845 to 1875, photographers presented their subjects in formal and refined images, while in the last quarter of the century they began to exploit the personal and illusionistic potential of photography. Illustrated by examples of nineteenth-century Philadelphia photography, these categories form a comparative framework that helps us better understand and appreciate the evolution of photographic intent.

PEOPLE

Within a few years after the introduction of the daguerreotype in Philadelphia, hundreds were made.[5] A few survive, some only as later reproductions of now-lost originals. During these early years the process was being improved and refined, and from extant pictures, it is evident that there was a struggle to align the potential of photography with proven image types. An obvious application was in portraiture.

Those who managed to join the process to this intent in the early months of the daguerreotype in Philadelphia were physician-chemist Paul Beck Goddard and brass founder Robert Cornelius. Portraiture had been considered only a dim possibility by Daguerre's advocate, François Arago, who believed that a breathing subject would make an unclear image. But Goddard's discovery that bromine helped make a plate more sensitive to light extended the daguerreotype into the realm of portraiture before December 1839, and by the following spring Cornelius had opened a studio at Eighth and Lodge Streets.[6] On May 15, Goddard presented two Cornelius daguerreotypes to the American Philosophical Society, portraits of Peter S. Du Ponceau, president of the Society (Fig. 2), and of John Vaughan, its treasurer.[7]

As a class of imagery, portraiture had a long history and strong traditions. In painted portraits, for example, there was an artistic sophistication founded upon cultural standards, the vanity of the sitter and the artist's desire for economic survival. Thomas Sully's idealization prevailed in a portrait of Du Ponceau painted nine years before the daguerreotype was made.[8] His projection of youth and spirit into the portrait of Du Ponceau at 70 was equivalent to his famous representations of middle-aged women as swan-necked beauties. Cornelius' daguerreotype of the same sitter, on the other hand, aimed simply at recognition. As Cornelius and others learned the constraints and the pos-

sibilities of their craft, they too generated rules and interpretations. The transition from representation to interpretation was accomplished within a decade by a few exceptional daguerrean artists.

Daguerreotypes were never shown at the annual exhibitions of the Pennsylvania Academy of Fine Arts but they were shown from 1843 on at the annual exhibitions of American manufactures sponsored by the Franklin Institute. This event concentrated on the progress of the mechanical arts and was supplemented by a small Fine Arts department, in which could be found a few paintings and drawings, prints, stained glass, window shades, silverware, examples of penmanship and daguerreotypes. Daguerrean entries of John Plumbe, Jr., William and Frederick Langenheim, Montgomery P. Simons, Marcus Aurelius Root, Samuel Van Loan, the firm of McClees and Germon and many others were honored year after year. In 1847, however, the Committee on Exhibitions expressed its bewilderment about daguerreotypes: "Although the judges do not consider this department as strictly belonging to the Fine Arts, still good collections of specimens are attractive and add to the interest of our exhibitions."[9] In the context of this uncertain status within the Fine Arts department, daguerreotype portraits by Root were given the highest award in 1848. One of these, depicting the young accountant Caleb C. Roberts, is still in the Franklin Institute (Fig. 3).[10]

Root was an energetic and a thoughtful portraitist who fully recognized the daguerrean art. In his treatise *The Camera and the Pencil*, published in 1864, Root argued with his less wide-awake colleagues that the human spirit was capable of transcending mere technique. He wrote that "sun-painting is *not* . . . a mere *mechanical* process . . . it is one of the fine arts . . . and in its *capabilities* is, at least, the *full equal* of the others bearing this name."[11] The responsibility of the "sun-painter" or "heliographer" was to prepare the sitter in pose and expression, relieve him of immediate concerns, and let the camera record the essence of the person as, Root believed, it would then be reflected in his appearance. Root intended to capture the twinkle in the sitter's eye. Referring to technical excellence, he continued: "Perfection itself . . . cannot even *begin* to fulfil the requisites of a true heliographic portrait, if it exhibits not that shadow of the soul which genius intuitively discerns, summons forth, and 'fixes.'"[12] In his conception of a portrait as the product of a skilled empathy with the subject, Root was the first daguerrean to define the esthetic aim in photography.

[5] No comprehensive survey has been undertaken to account for the surviving images made in the years of pre-professional photography.

[6] Daguerre, p. 30; *Proceedings of the American Philosophical Society*, Vol. 1, No. 9 (November and December 1839), p. 155.

[7] *Proceedings of the American Philosophical Society*, Vol. 1, No. 12 (May, June and July, 1840), p. 213.

[8] Thomas Sully's portrait of Peter S. Du Ponceau is owned by the American Philosophical Society, for which it was painted in March 1830.

[9] "Seventeenth Exhibition of American Manufactures, Report of the Committee on Exhibitions," *Journal of the Franklin Institute*, 44 (1847), p. 380.

[10] On the verso of the daguerreotype is a label with the inscription: "Taken by Marcus Aurelius Root/For/Franklin Institute Exhibition/Fall 1847/His Exhibit Took First Prize/over all competition." "Eighteenth Exhibition of American Manufactures, Report of the Committee on Exhibitions," *Journal of the Franklin Institute*, 46 (1848), p. 424.

[11] Root, p. 25.

[12] *Ibid.*, p. 144.

The standards of portraiture were refined by Root and his contemporaries in the 1840s and 1850s, and by the time of the Centennial, photographers had devised a full grammar of culture and decorum for their sitters. A sitter's picture was intended to project such appropriate inner qualities as intellect, boldness, generosity, gentility, humility and honor. When photographers could not find the desired characteristics on the subject's countenance, they often resorted to the use of props and fancy backgrounds, a practice Root considered untruthful.[13] At best, portraits made in Philadelphia from the mid-1840s through the 1870s presented a summary image of the sitter's public life.

The photograph of Walt Whitman attributed to Thomas Eakins (Fig. 4) dates from the early 1890s. Here we find no studio setting; the portrait was made in Whitman's Camden home. In this portrait we do not behold a great American poet; rather, we approach an inward-turned Whitman in his private place. The portrait is not a summary; the photographer did not aim to tell us all about the man. Compared with Root's studio portrait where Caleb C. Roberts is divorced from time and place, Whitman's photographer avoided such idealization to make the living poet real.[14]

The sheer ability of Cornelius, the technical and theoretical refinement of Root and the intense personal vision of Whitman's portraitist represent the evolution of photographic intent in portraiture. This outline is a basis for viewing and understanding other nineteenth-century portraits. And a similar three-part development is also found in the other classes of imagery.

PLACES

Soon after the new building of the Academy of Natural Sciences at Broad and Sansom Streets was opened in February 1840, a daguerreotype was made of the interior (Fig. 5). The lost original, probably by Paul Beck Goddard, was copied before 1900.[15] Goddard's use of bromine to make plates more light-sensitive, a discovery made simultaneously and independently by an Englishman with the same surname, broadened the application of the daguerreotype to portraiture and interior views.[16] Goddard's picture of the Academy of Natural Sciences indicates place by the singular presence of animal skeletons, just as the portrait of Du Ponceau is identified by his unique countenance. Such clear, unsophisticated images were the achievement of the early photographers.

Although the commercial success of portraiture had established a large market for the daguerreotype within a decade of its introduction, pictorial traditions for

places in paintings, engravings and such more recent print forms as aquatints, mezzotints and lithographs adapted less readily. A few daguerreotypes of places were inspired by advertising lithography of the 1840s. William G. Mason, a wood engraver on Chestnut Street near Second, photographed the optical and instrument store of his neighbor, John McAllister, Jr., in 1843 (Fig. 6). In the manner of contemporary lithographs, the well-dressed proprietor stands at the door of his establishment. Lithography remained the preferred medium for advertising, however; whereas the daguerreotype provided a strong and accurate image, a lithograph could eliminate all but the desired building, and could show it both inside and out, with employees tending customers, shifting stock and loading wagons. In addition to being more pictorial than daguerreotypes, lithographs were also larger and cheaper. Advertising photography did not become economically possible until the negative process and paper printing were firmly established in the 1850s.

The most striking photographs of places in mid-nineteenth-century Philadelphia are the antiquarian views by James E. McClees and Frederick DeBourg Richards in the 1850s and those by John Moran in the 1860s. The historic sites first photographed in 1853 were, among others, the London Coffee House, a pre-Revolutionary center of political and commercial decision making, and the Graff House, where Thomas Jefferson wrote the Declaration of Independence. By the 1860s, photographic antiquarianism included old and picturesque houses, barns, courts and graveyards—places sometimes more important to the nineteenth-century imagination than they had been in Colonial politics. Photographs of old and historic places commanded the respect felt at the sites themselves; this illusion was responsible for their popularity. Sentiment, the basic criterion in portraiture, also became the orientation for pictures of places.[17]

Antiquarian photographs were not issued in any particular form until 1859, when Richards was commissioned to photograph Germantown for an historical record that was to contain 20 prints with commentary by John Fanning Watson, the pioneer antiquarian of Philadelphia. Stereographs, twin photographs intended to be viewed with an illusion of three dimensions, were made of historic places and sold on a mammoth scale beginning around 1860. And in 1870 The Library Company of Philadelphia purchased a volume of 77 albumen prints by John Moran entitled *A Collection of Photographic Views in Philadelphia and its Vicinity.*[18] "603 Penn Street," a concise image of an

---

[13] *Ibid.*, p. 108.

[14] Many thanks to Dale Jensen for sharing his valuable insights on the photographs of Thomas Eakins.

[15] This is a gelatine print in the Free Library of Philadelphia, Castner Collection, Vol. 27a, p. 30.

[16] *Proceedings of the American Philosophical Society,* Vol. 3, No. 27 (May 25–30, 1843), p. 180; Josef Maria Eder, *History of Photography,* trans. by Edward Epstean, originally published 1945 (reprinted by Dover, 1978), pp. 265, 288.

[17] During a trip to the Middle East in 1849–51, French photographer Maxime Du Camp made paper negatives of monuments. One hundred and twenty-five were printed for the publication *Egypte, Nubie, Palestine et Syrie.* Henry Le Secq and Charles Nègre made photographs of French monuments for the government's Historical Monuments Commission early in the 1850s. Beaumont Newhall, *The History of Photography* (New York, The Museum of Modern Art, 1949), pp. 49–53.

[18] The Library Company of Philadelphia Folio Accession Book, number 1717, "bought from John Moran artist" [1870].

FIG. 3. Caleb C. Roberts. Half-plate daguerreotype by Marcus Aurelius Root, 1847.
The Franklin Institute.

FIG. 4. Walt Whitman. Gelatine print attributed to Thomas Eakins, ca. 1891. The Philadelphia Museum of Art (Bequest of Mark Lutz).

FIG. 5. Interior of the Academy of Natural Sciences. Gelatine print after a daguerreotype attributed to Paul Beck Goddard, ca. 1840. The Free Library of Philadelphia.

FIG. 6. "View of the houses Nos. 46, 48, 50 and 52, South side of Chestnut above 2nd St." Albumen print of 1862 after a sixth-plate daguerreotype by William G. Mason, June 17, 1843.

eighteenth-century row house from 1868, is one print in the Moran volume (Fig. 7). This facade composition is an expressive arrangement of doors and shutters upon the fine textures of a stone and brick wall. It is a still life constructed from an unlikely perspective and, in its distance from usual experience, restrains the illusion of reality.

Antiquarian photographs from the 1850s and 1860s have a clarity and an intensity not found in the work of Goddard or Mason. Expectations in photographs of places by McClees, Richards and Moran were similar to Root's expectations in portraiture. Moran's preference for concise imagery was voiced at a meeting of the Philadelphia Photographic Society in February 1865. He stated that "any given scene offers so many different points of view, but if there is not the perceiving mind to note and feel the relative degrees of importance in the various aspects which nature presents, nothing worthy the name of pictures can be produced."[19] Moran, Root and their contemporaries intended to bare the essence of their subjects, whatever the material form, in photographs beautiful as objects. Their direct and plain kind of imagery might be called classical photography.

On a winter Sunday in 1880, S. Fisher Corlies made a photograph at the Library Company building on Fifth Street (Fig. 8). The pictured room contained the library of James Logan, classical scholar and secretary to William Penn. When Corlies made the photograph, some of the books had been moved to the new library building at Broad and Christian Streets, but in spite of the bare shelves, the room is light and warm. Chairs, tables and books are props on Corlies' "stage," which generates an unrestrained illusion. We see the room at eye level, as if we were there. As we project our imagination into Corlies' picture, the sunlit chair in its center invites us to experience the sensations associated with an historical library.

A comparison of the photographs of Moran and Corlies reveals two very different intentions. Moran's concise presentation of the unknown house is complete in itself. Corlies developed an illusion of a well-known library. Moran is formal and disciplined; Corlies is informal and romantic. In the later period, the essence of the subject is not presented in the image, but rather cultivated in the mind of the viewer: our imaginative response to Corlies' photograph is to recollect the musty smell of leather bindings. Corlies' library, like the Whitman portrait, molds impressions rather than imposing an interpretation.

OBJECTS

In 1840, at the age of 16, Mathew Carey Lea made prints of his botanical specimen collection on light-sensitive paper. His father, Isaac Lea, a famous naturalist and publisher, exhibited the work at meetings of the

American Philosophical Society in February of that year.[20] In 1841, 233 unique prints were organized by botanical class, bound and entitled *Photogenic Drawings of Plants Indigenous to the Vicinity of Philadelphia*. An example of the class Hexandria is a print of *Lilium philadelphicum*, a plant discovered by eighteenth-century botanist John Bartram (Fig. 9). As with early photographic images of people and places, Lea also established a simple identifiable impression.

Twenty-seven years later, John Moran photographed a chair thought to have been owned by William Penn. "Penn Chair" (Fig. 10) is an albumen print from the same volume as "603 Penn Street." Most likely, the chair was not Penn's; it was one of many English chairs dating from the turn of the eighteenth century to which American owners attached a distinguished provenance. But it was Penn's in Moran's mind, and in his presentation of its image.

The chair was brought out-of-doors and raised on overturned pots. Its presentation is plain, frontal, still and distant; it thus shares the formal qualities evident in "603 Penn Street" and Root's "Caleb C. Roberts." The chair is a relic; even without a title, its image would proclaim importance. We are not made welcome to sit on the chair, as we are not invited to enter 603 Penn Street or to converse with Caleb C. Roberts. Moran wrote: ". . . in looking at works of art we see not alone with the eyes; the object must be illuminated from within; otherwise all things, whether of nature or art, are but dead, inanimate matter."[21] In "Penn Chair," Moran revealed the object's essence, just as Root reflected the sitter's soul in portraits.

The Centennial Exposition opened in 1876 and Philadelphia invited the world to see the triumph of American arts and manufactures. On opening day, May 10, 1876, President Grant spoke briefly, then led a procession of four thousand persons through the Main Building and into Machinery Hall. The most thrilling exhibit in the hall was its centerpiece: the steam engine invented and manufactured by George H. Corliss of Providence, Rhode Island. Corliss stood by his engine and instructed the President and Emperor Dom Pedro II of Brazil to turn two levers. Hundreds of mechanical exhibits were set into motion; the thousands cheered.

The photograph, like the engine, is imposing: 17 by 21 inches, the largest offered by William Notman and the Centennial Photographic Company (Fig. 11). In it, we are invited to marvel at the size and spectacle: the whirring and grinding, the smell of oil, the vibrating ground. Without this imaginary experience, which depends upon our awareness of the Centennial, the print would be no more than a brownish image of a large machine. Unlike Moran's work, the picture "Corliss

---

[19] John Moran, "The Relation of Photography to the Fine Arts," *The Philadelphia Photographer*, Vol. 2, No. 15 (March 1865), p. 33; Moran seemed to use Root's perspectives as a point of departure.

[20] At a meeting of February 6, 1840, "Mr. Lea exhibited nearly forty specimens of representations of plants and shells, by the photographic process of Talbot, modified by Mr. Mungo Ponton of Edinburgh . . . prepared by his son Mr. Carey Lea." *Proceedings of the American Philosophical Society*, Vol. 1, No. 10 (1840), pp. 171, 177.

[21] Moran, p. 35.

Engine" is not a lovely object. It is poster-like, mounted without a border, its title affixed to the face of the print. Moreover, by contrast with Moran's "Penn Chair," our experience of the photograph creates the illusion of our presence in Machinery Hall.

From the middle of the 1840s through the 1860s, photographers were artisans whose products were wonderful to behold as objects and images. Their photographs were decorous and delightful, joining cultural and personal values. Photographs from the later period were sensational illustrations, often made by the thousands, as we can see from the Centennial Photographic Company catalogues. The style of a photographer like Moran would have no place in such an industry. In the photographs by William Notman and his staff, meaningful illusions replaced the refined pictorial conservatism of the earlier decades.

EVENTS

Not long before the Nativist Party riots in Philadelphia, William and Frederick Langenheim opened a portraiture studio in the Merchants' Exchange building. On the evening of May 8, 1844, the Catholic churches of St. Michael and St. Augustine were burned by Know-Nothing mobs. The next morning Major-General Patterson of the Pennsylvania Militia established headquarters in the Girard Bank building, just a few blocks to the south of the rioting. A window of the Merchants' Exchange provided an excellent view of the military occupation, and the Langenheims took the opportunity to make a whole-plate daguerreotype of the event (Fig. 12).

In May of 1856, James E. McClees photographed the smoldering ruins after a severe fire of homes and businesses in the vicinity of Independence Hall (Fig. 13). Buildings on the same block of Chestnut Street as McClees's studio had been destroyed. In order to photograph the ruins (two different views are known), McClees found a perch in a surviving building to the northwest of Independence Hall, which is partially visible through the conflagration. McClees's print is an account of mid-nineteenth-century pyrophobia: a sentiment reflected in the image of one disaster.

The Gilliams and Stratton Syndicate photographed street scenes in the mid-1890s. An albumen print of a market entitled "On South Street," attributed to Leslie E. Gilliams and Richard C. Stratton, is typical of photographs from the later period (Fig. 14). Unlike the Langenheims and McClees, the photographer was in the very scene he photographed. And by contrast with the succinct historicism of the earlier prints, "On South Street" depicts an everyday event. Since its photographer provided no historical message, we draw from our impressions of street markets and supply our own interpretation. Where the Langenheim's daguerreotype is a "presentation" image of a unique event, and McClees's print an abstraction of one, "On South Street" permits entrance into a portion of daily life.

VIEWS

The content in photographs of the previous four classes of imagery—people, places, objects and events—is specific and limited. In those of the fifth class, views, a topographical or urban context is presented. An early example is Joseph Saxton's daguerreotype made in October 1839 (Fig. 1). The buildings in the image, an arsenal and Central High School, were not the intended subjects. Rather, Saxton was interested in reproducing a recognizable portion of the city.

Showmanship is evident in the six half-plate daguerreotype panorama by Thomas P. and David C. Collins entitled "Fairmount Water Works" (Fig. 15). The 1846 panorama, produced soon after the photographers opened a portrait studio on Chestnut Street, was a demonstration of their daguerrean abilities. It was intended for exhibition, the plates being mounted behind a gold-velvet panel with brass decorations and labels with the title and makers' names in large type. The scale, rich colors and textures alone make the panorama impressive, and the self-conscious illusion that we are really opposite the Fairmount Water Works makes this version of a famous prospect of Philadelphia complete and exciting.

The Collins view, like the examples by Root, Moran and McClees in the other categories, broadened the expectations of mid-century photography. Root demanded that a portrait should emphasize the best qualities of the sitter; a portrait of Daniel Webster, for instance, should show him as an orator because oration served "to rouse his entire nature into the intensest activity."[22] In the 1840s, the Fairmount Water Works was the definitive view of Philadelphia; it typified the city's public image in the same way that Root's portraits were summaries of the public lives of his sitters.

Nearly 50 years later, on July 4, 1893, William Nicholson Jennings ascended in a balloon from Fairmount Park with the famed aeronaut Samuel A. King. "Balloon View of Philadelphia from a point one mile high," one of the several pictures made on the occasion of that trip, shows the greater part of North Philadelphia through the haze that had confounded previous aerial photographers (Fig. 16). The results especially surprised King, who had been a confirmed skeptic in regard to aerial photography. In financial difficulties, King had approached Jennings for a loan to finance this balloon trip in return for the photographic opportunity. The ascension was later recalled by Jennings:

On the Fourth of July, when the word was given to "let go" and the "Eagle Eyrie" bore this cameraman and a fellow passenger aloft, the Municipal Band struck up "My Sweetheart's the Man in the Moon" and the immense crowd of up-lookers were squeezed together and evaporated; there being no sense on our part of rising; the earth seemed to be sinking and slowly sliding beneath us.[23]

[22] Root, p. 157.
[23] W. N. Jennings, "Snapshots From Cloudland," *Journal of the Franklin Institute*, 218, No. 6 (December 1934), pp. 670–671.

FIG. 7. "603 Penn St.—1868." Albumen print by John Moran.

FIG. 8. "Back room in the old library building in Fifth Street below Chestnut Street in which was kept the 'Loganian Library.'" Albumen print by S. Fisher Corlies, 1880.

FIG. 9. "Lilium Philadelphicum." Photogenic drawing by Mathew Carey Lea, ca. 1840. The Franklin Institute.

FIG. 10. "Penn Chair." Albumen print by John Moran, ca. 1868.

FIG. 11. "Corliss Engine," Machinery Hall. Albumen print by the Centennial Photographic Company, 1876. 17 × 21 inches. The Free Library of Philadelphia.

FIG. 12. "North-East corner of Third and Dock street, Girard Bank, at the time the
latter was occupied by the Military during the riots." Whole-plate daguerreotype
by William and Frederick Langenheim, May 9, 1844.

FIG. 13. "View of the ruins caused by the great fire Northeast corner of Sixth and Market st. which began on the night of Weds. April 30, 1856—From the Northeast." Albumenized salt print by James E. McClees.

FIG. 14. "On South Street." Albumen print attributed to the Gilliams and Stratton Syndicate, ca. 1896. The Historical Society of Pennsylvania.

FIG. 15. "Fairmount Water Works." Six half-plate daguerreotypes by Thomas P. and David C. Collins, ca. 1846. The Franklin Institute.

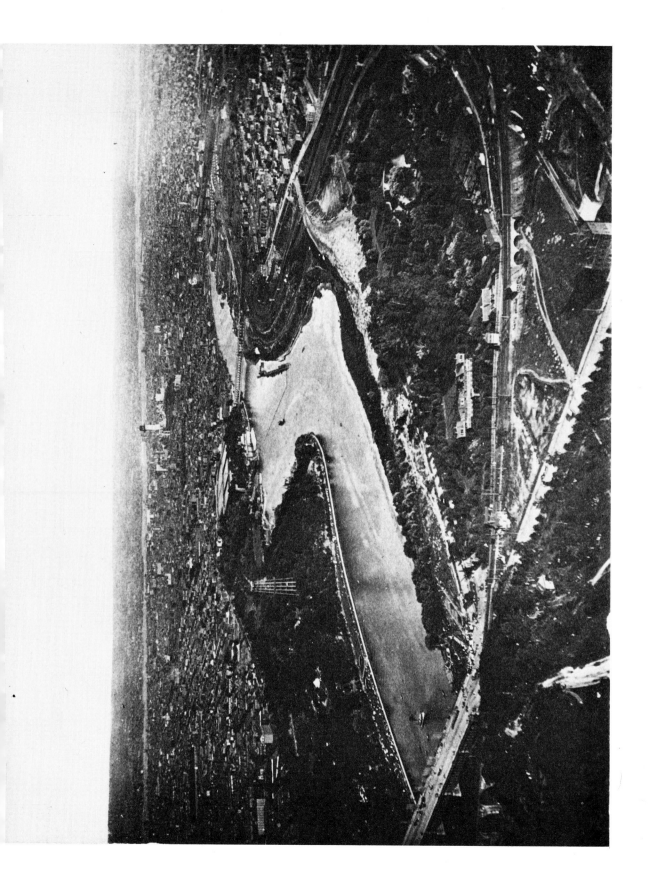

FIG. 16. "Balloon View of Philadelphia from a point one mile high." Gelatine print by W. N. Jennings, July 4, 1893. The Historical Society of Pennsylvania.

For years, Jennings had experimented with various plates and filters in anticipation of this first attempt at aerial photography from a balloon. Using his 6½-by-8½ inch camera at the height of a mile, he produced "sharp, crisp, clear-cut negatives." Unlike the Collins panorama, which is a presentation view of Philadelphia, Jennings' photograph is an illustration of his adventure. It is a visual accompaniment to a story that would otherwise have been incomplete. "Balloon View of Philadelphia" engages our imagination and makes us want to look beyond its borders to see the rest of the city.

The Saxton view has a fixed place in the history of photography. The Collins view is a well-constructed, unique and cultured package, the epitome of mid-century imagery. Having few obligations to such standards in 1893, a time when artists and writers were cultivating ideas that were the foundation of twentieth-century subjective imagery, Jennings made a view that is incomplete without its narrative. Once again, the expectations of photography in Philadelphia during the nineteenth century were in three stages: the impression, the presentation and the illusion.

CONCLUSION

The study of nineteenth-century photography is still very new. As the body of knowledge grows, choices are made. Certain photographers become preferred and single prints are chosen to represent entire movements. To lay the groundwork for these decisions, large numbers of images must be assembled, compared and considered. Our stubborn biases must be uprooted, allowing photography to thrive in its historical context.

The work for historians becomes evident. Photographers with fertile careers distinguish themselves; their monographs beg to be written. Esoteric techniques demand study. Comparisons that were once considered overly subtle become fruitful with new insights. Previously unseen work can be evaluated with assurance, paving the way to new discoveries. This is the way toward an understanding of early photography; and to proceed we must simply look, think and enjoy.

NINETEENTH-CENTURY PHOTOGRAPHY IN PHILADELPHIA

PEOPLE

POLITICIANS AND BUSINESSMEN
(Illustrations 1–5)

In 1884, Scharf and Westcott wrote of Richard Vaux: "He has led an active political life of over forty years, and yet no one can point to any act of his and say that its motive was not as stainless as the Arctic snow." Vaux was admitted to the bar in 1837 and served, at various times, as diplomat, penologist, educator and mayor. He declined support from the Nativists in the Philadelphia mayoral race of 1845, rejecting their demand for a native-born police force. Vaux lost that election and another in 1854, but in 1856, at the age of 40 he finally won. An unpretentious portrait of the "Bourbon warhorse" mayor was made by Frederick DeBourg Richards and [John] Betts.

Morton McMichael, mayor from 1866 to 1869, was photographed for *Representative Men of Philadelphia,* a collection of 87 portraits made during the Centennial by W. Curtis Taylor of the firm Broadbent and Taylor. McMichael, one of the "Philadelphians worthily representing the Industry, Enterprise and Intellect of the City in the nation's Centennial Year," had been editor of numerous publications since the 1820s, including the *Saturday Evening Post* and the Philadelphia *North American,* which he owned by 1854. As police magistrate, McMichael began his political life when he prevented a mob from burning an orphanage for black children in 1837. His diplomatic skills were an asset to Philadelphia again during the Native American riots of 1844, and McMichael continued to serve as a civic leader through the 1870s.

Others selected for Taylor's *Representative Men* were James Joseph Barclay, founder and director of the House of Refuge, a home for vagrant children, and John Wanamaker, the merchant whose keen use of newspaper advertising made him a wealthy man and his department store a Philadelphia institution. An earlier meteoric rise to fortune was witnessed in the life of Dr. David Jayne, a promoter of patent medicines who advertised his wares worldwide. Within two decades his success created a business that occupied a grandiose new eight-story granite building on Chestnut Street, finished in 1850. The tower of this structure burned in a spectacular fire in 1872 (Ill. 160), six years after Jayne's death.

CLERGY
(Illustrations 6–9)

One of Philadelphia's earliest carte-de-visite photographs was of the 90-year-old Benjamin Dorr, rector of Christ Church since 1837. Washington Lafayette Germon copyrighted this portrait in 1859, a common practice when the subject was well known. Three years later this most economical of all photographic formats was being produced by the thousands. Frederick Gutekunst's contribution included a portrait of Alexander Crummell, American leader of a movement for the westernization of Africa. Crummell had been rebuffed by the American Protestant Episcopal establishment in the 1840s and, after receiving a degree from Cambridge, assumed a professorship at the College of Liberia. By the 1880s Crummell returned to the United States and, finally recognized for his leadership, became rector of St. Luke's Church in Washington, D.C. W. E. B. DuBois wrote of Crummell in 1903: "Some seer he seemed, that came not from the crimson Past or the grey To-come, but from the pulsing Now—that mocking world which seemed to me at once so light and dark, so splendid and sordid."

One of Crummell's early antagonists was Henry Ustick Onderdonk, the Episcopal bishop of Pennsylvania. Onderdonk offered to bring Crummell into his diocese on condition that he would never ask for representation at church conventions. Crummell refused, choosing rather to work at an impoverished church in New York. Though other aspects of Onderdonk's work were respected, a tendency to overindulge in drink led to voluntary resignation in 1844. Rehabilitation and good work brought his reinstatement in 1856, and it was shortly later that this portrait was made.

One of the city's earliest daguerreans, Montgomery P. Simons (credited with the Onderdonk portrait) wrote in 1857 that "photography on paper is, beyond all controversy, the highest state of the 'Heliographic Art,' yet it does not . . . come into competition with the daguerreotype." Simons' reliance upon the luminous depths that the earlier silver plate had given images is evident in the plainness of the Onderdonk portrait, which is on paper. Handsome but less profound portraits were made by such latecomers to the photographic community as Samuel Broadbent, whose commercially successful formula, employing dress, props and pose, made a gentlemanly statement in the portrait of Joseph T. Cooper, pastor of the Second Associate Presbyterian Church.

VARIOUS CELEBRITIES
(Illustrations 10–13)

Perhaps a dozen mid-century Philadelphians were situated comfortably enough to turn from their trades to antiquarianism. John McAllister, Jr. became the most dedicated of these men. In 1835, at the age of 49, he began devoting his time to collecting letters, pictures and books about Philadelphia and its people. His investigations, which provided factual substantiation of historical anecdotes, often appeared as newspaper articles. It was McAllister who established the fact that Jefferson drafted the Declaration of Independence at the Graff House. Guided by his influence, the McAllister family turned to photographic publishing around 1859, listing thousands of lantern slides and stereographs in their catalogues. McAllister knew photographers and collected their work. According to Root, he insisted upon being the first commercial sitter for daguerrean Robert Cornelius. And in 1843, he had wood engraver and daguerrean William G. Mason make a series of plates of his Chestnut Street building, which he proudly noted "had the largest 'shop window' in Philadelphia" (see Fig. 6 in the Introduction). In the 1890s, his son, John A. McAllister, donated the bulk of the family collection to The Library Company of Philadelphia.

Magician Antonio Blitz performed throughout Europe before his fifteenth birthday. His acts of ventriloquism stunned audiences and, though accused of collusion with the devil, Blitz was widely imitated. He settled in Philadelphia in 1859 and worked with Dr. Thomas Kirkbride at the Asylum of Pennsylvania Hospital. Kirkbride also engaged the Langenheim brothers, Blitz's portraitists, to present lantern slides to the same patients.

Lucretia Coffin Mott was an independent Friend and a reformer whose strength and calm won the respect of Emerson and Thoreau. Her anti-slavery convictions influenced her husband James to abandon his profitable trade with slaveholders, and their home soon became a station for the Underground Railroad. Mrs. Mott was present at the founding of the American Anti-Slavery Society in Philadelphia in 1833, and helped found the Philadelphia Female Anti-Slavery Society. She was outspoken in the causes of temperance, women's rights and peace.

Hebrew poet Naphtali Herz Imber left his native Galicia at the age of 15. While in Rumania in 1878 he wrote "Hatikvah," a Zionist poem later adopted as Israel's national anthem. He joined a small settlement in Haifa and worked as the secretary to its leader, Laurence Oliphant. After Oliphant's death in 1888, Imber went to England and a few years later arrived in the United States. He eventually settled in New York City, where a stipend from a wealthy friend allowed the continuation of his work in literature and mysticism. Imber was a bohemian, with a devotion to the occult, a propensity to drink and a disdain for authority.

Elias Goldensky, Imber's photographer, would have found his subject impossible to portray in the literal manner so often employed in the nineteenth century. The portrait of McAllister, by contrast—a confidently posed gentleman amidst his collected scientific apparatus—is just such a literal description. Imber's portrait represents a purer and a more modern visual language. Goldensky found in Imber a photographic opportunity: a man at the periphery of society yet at the heart of the human spirit.

PHOTOGRAPHERS
(Illustrations 14–23)

Not one month after Parisians witnessed the photochemical triumph of Daguerre, disbelieving Americans were anxious for proof. In September 1839, Alexander Dallas Bache, great-grandson of Benjamin Franklin and chief of research at the Institute bearing his ancestor's name, published in its journal a brief article entitled "The Daguerreotype Explained." It was hardly enough of an explanation to encourage an American product, and a full translation of Daguerre's own description appeared in the November issue. Its translator was John Fries Frazer, who later succeeded Bache at the Franklin Institute and in the chair of chemistry and natural philosophy at the University of Pennsylvania. Out of curiosity, or scepticism, Frazer made a daguerreotype himself, according to Marcus Aurelius Root, who is credited with a later portrait of the pioneer daguerrean.

Paul Beck Goddard was an anatomist and a colleague of Bache and Frazer. While assistant to University of Pennsylvania Professor of Chemistry Robert Hare in the fall of 1839, Goddard discovered that bromine vapor made a daguerreotype more light-sensitive. His experiments were simultaneous with and identical to those of the Englishman John Frederick Goddard, whose champions later hoped to deprive the Philadelphian of his claim.

M. A. Root was an early chronicler of this and of other debates of the daguerrean era, which he more than a little influenced. Root claimed for his Fifth and Chestnut Street studio over 70,000 subjects. In spite of this output, dozens of other daguerreans thrived. German-born competitors William and Frederick Langenheim, located in the Merchants' Exchange Building, made portraits of such luminaries as Jackson, Webster and Clay. The Langenheim brothers had gained an international reputation in 1845, when they sent to European royalty the first daguerreotypes of Niagara Falls. Their enthusiasm for technical improvement brought Voigtländer lenses, the talbotype and the stereograph to the United States. Root was more inclined to theory. His *Camera and the Pencil* of 1864 is a treatise on the history, practice and potential of photography. In it, Root defined the portrait-maker's responsibility: "The sitter, before a transcript of him is taken, should be put into a *mood,* which shall make his face *diaphanous* with expression of his highest and best i.e., his *genuine, essential self.*" Painters had long known that the appropriate topic of conversation brought expression to a sitter's face and Root emphasized this principle for photography.

Frederick Debourg Richards was a painter who found a career in photography beginning in the late 1840s. His volume of clients was hardly that of Root's or the Langenheims', but his work competed with theirs for prizes at annual exhibitions of the Institute of American Manufactures. Richards was one of the city's early paper photographers—over 150 of his pre-1860 views are known. But photography lost its innocence about the time of the Civil War and Richards returned to painting.

Proliferation after 1860 also meant a corps of amateur photographers. The Philadelphia Photographic Exchange Club and the Philadelphia Photographic Society were both spawned during that period. Many of their devotees were old-family Philadelphians, such as John C. Browne and S. Fisher Corlies. In their work the fading values of early photography were maintained.

Nineteenth-century photography became a business like any other, and no one succeeded at it quite like Frederick Gutekunst, who had organ music played for his waiting patrons. Gutekunst produced cartes-de-visite by the thousands, claimed to have made the "world's largest" photograph at the Centennial, and built up a photo-reproduction business at his Arch Street premises. William H. Rau entered the field just before the Centennial, William N. Jennings a decade later. Both of these men, with Gutekunst, carried nineteenth-century notions of commercial photography into the twentieth century. This they tempered with dedication to the medium: Rau was an entrant in the 1898 Philadelphia Photographic Salon, and Jennings was a founder, with Louis Walton Sipley in 1938, of the first museum of photography.

PAINTERS AND PRINTMAKERS
(Illustrations 24–34)

Philadelphia was an active center of American art in the nineteenth century between the well-known achievements of Charles Willson Peale and Thomas Eakins. But there was a creative pause during the mid-century, as a prolific community of artists was occupied in satisfying the demands of a culturally ambitious middle class. For the most part, these painters and printmakers had only local reputations and, for a time, Philadelphia had little influence upon the direction of American art.

As a group, painters tolerated photography. Rembrandt Peale wrote in 1857 that the daguerreotype "has certainly killed *bad* miniature painting, but it cannot supersede portrait painting, though it may . . . interfere with its encouragement." It was common practice for printmakers to copy daguerreotype portraits: Albert Newsam and John Sartain did so voluminously in lithograph and mezzotint, respectively. Many painters were also photographers: Frederick DeBourg Richards, John Moran, Frederick A. Wenderoth and Isaac Rehn turned from palette to camera, and often back again. Parallels between late-century painting and photography are evident in the marine-scape cyanotypes and watercolors of Richards; others have been revealed in the work of Thomas Eakins. Eadweard Muybridge's massive photographic project for *Animal Locomotion* of the 1880s had Eakins on its supervisory committee. For the 11-volume study Muybridge used banks of still cameras to capture subleties of movement and expression in sequence. His work was on the common frontier of art and science and had a hearty influence on the development of modern vision.

MISCELLANEOUS
(Illustrations 35–53)

Precious few of the vast numbers of portraits made in nineteenth-century Philadelphia still bear identification of their subjects. Respect is due these miscellaneous and now nameless pictures; many are outstanding examples of a burgeoning photographic business. The city directories account for over 300 studios at various times before 1870. And the portraitists' livelihood depended upon a full waiting room of well-dressed sitters-to-be. A few dozen examples rise above the thousands. These daguerreotypes, ambrotypes, prints and cartes-de-visite carried on the standards for which their makers became known.

1. Richard Vaux, 1816–1895. Salt print by Frederick DeBourg Richards and [John] Betts, ca.1856.

2. Morton McMichael, 1807–1879. Albumen print by W. Curtis Taylor, 1876.

3. James J. Barclay, 1794–1885. Albumen print by W. Curtis Taylor, 1876.

4. John Wanamaker, 1838–1922. Albumen print by W. Curtis Taylor, 1876.

5. Dr. David Jayne, 1799–1866. Salt print by an unidentified photographer, ca.1858.

LEFT: **6.** Benjamin Dorr, 1769–1869. Albumen-print carte-de-visite by Washington Lafayette Germon, 1859. RIGHT: **7.** Alexander Crummell, 1819–1898. Albumen-print carte-de-visite by Frederick Gutekunst, 1862.

8. Henry Ustick Onderdonk, 1789–1858. Salt print attributed to Montgomery P. Simons, ca.1858.

9. Joseph T. Cooper. Salt print by Samuel Broadbent, 1858.

TOP: **10.** John McAllister, Jr., 1786–1877. Albumen-print stereograph attributed to William and Frederick Langenheim, ca.1860. BOTTOM: **11.** "Signor Blitz, from life." Antonio Blitz, 1810–1877. Albumen-print stereograph by William and Frederick Langenheim, ca.1860.

12. Lucretia Coffin Mott, 1793–1880. Albumen-print stereograph attributed to Frederick Gutekunst, ca.1862.

13. Naphtali Herz Imber, 1856–1909. Gum-bichromate print by Elias Goldensky, ca.1904.

14. John Fries Frazer, 1812–1872. Half-plate daguerreotype attributed to Marcus
Aurelius Root, ca. 1850.

TOP LEFT: **15.** Paul Beck Goddard, M.D., 1811–1866. Albumen-print carte-de-visite by Frederick Gutekunst, 1862. TOP RIGHT: **16.** Marcus Aurelius Root, 1808–1888. Albumen-print carte-de-visite by an unidentified photographer, ca. 1864. BOTTOM: **17.** William Langenheim, 1807–1874. Salt print attributed to the Langenheim studio, ca. 1860.

18. Frederick DeBourg Richards, 1822–1903. Salt print, attributed self-portrait, ca. 1860. The Historical Society of Pennsylvania.

LEFT: **19.** John C. Browne, 1838–1918. Albumen-print carte-de-visite by an unidentified photographer, ca. 1865. RIGHT: **20.** S. Fisher Corlies, 1830–1888. Albumen-print carte-de-visite by an unidentified photographer, ca. 1863.

21. Frederick Gutekunst, 1831–1917. Platinum print attributed to the Gutekunst studio, ca. 1905. The Historical Society of Pennsylvania.

22. William H. Rau, 1855–1920. Silver print, attributed self-portrait, ca. 1918.

23. William Nicholson Jennings, 1860–1946. Silver print, attributed self-portrait, ca. 1930.

24. Philadelphia Painters. Members of the Artists' Fund Society. Bottom row, left to right: unidentified; Newbold H. Trotter, 1827–1898; [Thomas Moran, 1837–1926]; [Edmund Darch Lewis, 1835–1910]. Middle row: George Washington Conarroe, 1802–1886; George W. Pettit; James Reid Lambdin, 1807–1889; Frederick DeBourg Richards, 1822–1903; John Sartain, 1808–1897. Top row: unidentified; unidentified; Isaac L. Williams, 1817–1895. Albumen print by an unidentified photographer, ca. 1885.

25. Albert Newsam, 1809–1874. Salt print by Walter Dinmore, ca. 1859.

26. John Sartain, 1808–1897. Albumen print by W. Curtis Taylor, 1876.

27. Thomas Sully, 1783–1872. Salt print by an unidentified photographer, ca. 1857.

28. Thomas Sully in His Studio. Albumen-print stereograph by an unidentified photographer, ca. 1862.

LEFT: **29.** George Washington Conarroe, 1802–1886. Half-plate daguerreotype by Frederick DeBourg Richards, ca. 1857. RIGHT: **30.** James Reid Lambdin, 1807–1889. Albumen print by an unidentified photographer, ca. 1863.

31. Edward Moran, 1829–1901. Salt print by an unidentified photographer, ca. 1859.

32. William Trost Richards (1833–1905) in His Studio. Albumen print by an unidentified photographer, ca. 1862.

33. Edmund Darch Lewis, 1835–1910. Albumen print by W. Curtis Taylor, 1876.

34. ''Scenery in the Region of the Delaware Water Gap, Pennsylvania. Delaware River, from Prospect Rock.'' Albumen-print stereograph by Moran and [?] Storey, ca. 1864.

35. Pennsylvania Militiaman. Whole-plate daguerreotype by Marcus Aurelius
Root, ca. 1846.

36. Man with Shawl. Salt print by an unidentified photographer, ca. 1858.

37. Standing Woman. Salt print by James E. McClees, ca. 1856.

38. Seated Woman. Half-plate daguerreotype by Marcus Aurelius Root, ca. 1846.

39. Seated Man. Half-plate daguerreotype by Marcus Aurelius Root, ca. 1846.

40. Man and Elderly Woman. Half-plate daguerreotype by Montgomery P. Simons, ca. 1847.

41. Charlotte Biddle West Conarroe and Daughter. Quarter-plate daguerreotype by Frederick DeBourg Richards, ca. 1857.

42. Two Sisters. Quarter-plate ambrotype by Isaac Rehn, ca. 1854.

43. Children with Tent. Albumen print attributed to Coonley and Wolfersberger,
ca. 1862.

44. ''Liny Borie, 2 years—2 months old.'' Half-plate daguerreotype by William and Frederick Langenheim, ca. 1846.

45. "Georgie. Edwin. Abram. Hamil. Grubb. Orville. James. Neddie." Salt print by Frederick Gutekunst in *The Mind Unveiled; or a brief history of twenty-two Imbecile Children* (Philadelphia: U. Hunt & Son, 1858).

46. Standing Man. Albumen print attributed to Coonley and Wolfersberger, ca. 1862.

LEFT: **47.** Soldier with Rifle. Albumen-print carte-de-visite by Frederick Gutekunst, ca. 1864. RIGHT: **48.** Seated Soldier. Albumen-print carte-de-visite by Wenderoth and Taylor, ca. 1864.

49. Clement Biddle Barclay, 1817–1896. Albumen print attributed to John C. Browne, ca. 1865.

50. Group of Women in the Pennsylvania Academy of Fine Arts. Albumen-print stereograph by an unidentified photographer, ca. 1864.

51. "Photographed at night by the Magnesium Light   Dec. 1865   J.C.B." Albumen print by John C. Browne.

52. [Hand keeping time.] Plate 535 from *Animal Locomotion*, Philadelphia, 1887 (reprint: Dover, 1979). Collotype after photographs by Eadweard Muybridge.

53. Liberty. Autochrome by William H. Rau, ca. 1910.

PLACES

OLD HOUSES
(Illustrations 54–68)

Houses of important eighteenth-century people often appeared inappropriate in the midst of commercial nineteenth-century Philadelphia. The city's oldest parts were being engulfed by the newer and larger cast-iron structures for prospering industry. As the homes of venerated historical figures vanished, Philadelphia's presentt and past became irreconcilable. Antiquarians collected stories that had once been common knowledge and encouraged photographers and printmakers to record buildings that were formerly well-known sights.

Quaint accounts of Philadelphia lore and history accompany such pictures of "ancient dwellings" as the 1854 print by Frederick DeBourg Richards, "William Penn's Mansion, or the 'Slate-roof house.'" Finished in 1700, the U-shaped house on Second Street above Walnut was home to a succession of families prominent in business and politics. William and Hannah Penn's son John was born there. James Logan, the proprietor's secretary, entertained there. The house was purchased by William Trent, founder of Trenton, by the Norris family, then by Governor James Hamilton. By the time of the first Continental Congress in 1774 it had become a boarding house where John Adams and others stayed. During a sharp comedown in the nineteenth century as a shop and a sawmill with a wooden addition between its wings, the Slate Roof House survived several threats until 1868, when it was removed to make way for the Commercial Exchange Building.

Builder Benjamin Loxley's 1760 house, on Second Street below Spruce, developed a reputation from the military involvements of its eighteenth-century occupants. Captain Loxley would have been in charge of the battle with the Paxton Boys in 1764 had Franklin failed to convince the group of more than a thousand to abandon their intentions to enter Philadelphia and massacre Indians sheltered in the Courthouse. Loxley served through the Revolution, during which Lydia Darragh lived in the house. She became a posthumous heroine when an account of a deed of hers emerged in 1827. Upon overhearing British officers secretly planning an attack on Washington's Whitemarsh encampment, she successfully had the General warned.

Cliveden, the country seat of Chief Justice Benjamin Chew and site of the Battle of Germantown, survives today thanks to its semirural location. Many city houses were photographed shortly before they were pulled down. The "Old wooden houses" on Tenth Street above Chestnut were removed to make way for the Franklin Market, just after Richards made the photograph in March 1859. The mansion built for lawyer Edward Shippen Burd in 1801 by Benjamin Henry Latrobe was photographed after the death of his widow, Eliza Sims Burd, in 1860. The building was removed two years later (Ill. 197).

John McAllister, Jr., collector of facts as well as photographs, established in 1855 that Thomas Jefferson drafted the Declaration of Independence in the Jacob Graff house at Seventh and Market Streets. Jefferson rented the entire second floor beginning in May 1776 and, it was determined, wrote in the front room. That location was soon distinguished by an awning, doubtless in patriotic colors, proclaiming it the "Birth Place of Liberty." The house was eventually torn down, though replaced with a facsimile in 1976.

In a similar but more esoteric expression of topophilia, John Moran visited and photographed the birthplace of Benjamin West in 1869. Successor to Joshua Reynolds as president of the Royal Academy, West had a firm influence upon many nineteenth-century artists, including the English-born Moran brothers. West is buried in Saint Paul's Cathedral, a jolting contrast to the Springfield, Pennsylvania farmhouse. Such romantic allusions were Moran's style.

Precedents for Moran's antiquarian spirit had been established by Richards and Odiorne, and survived with their long-active amateur contemporary John C. Browne. The evolving antiquarian tradition is represented in Odiorne's 1860 "Little Dock & Spruce," showing a site just across from the Loxley House. Later in the same decade, Moran searched out the city's most picturesque and sometimes obscure eighteenth-century dwellings. Twenty years later, Browne continued to make photographic jaunts to the remaining historic houses on the city's periphery.

OLD PUBLIC BUILDINGS
(Illustrations 69–80)

On one occasion in 1811, while English-born and educated William Staughton was preaching at Philadelphia's First Baptist Church, the hall became laden with smoke. "There must be an Englishman in the stovepipe," remarked the sexton. Such open resentment of Staughton, which reflected the tense Anglo-American relations before the War of 1812, precipitated a division within the congregation. "Dr. Staughton's Baptist Church," built for the dissidents by architect Robert Mills, soon opened on Sansom Street and grew in popularity until he left in the early 1820s. A few years before the building was torn down, Frederick DeBourg Richards photographed it as seen over the foundations of the Continental Hotel.

Staughton's church stood slightly longer than did the Jersey Market Terminus, built in 1822 and pulled down in 1859. Henry B. Odiorne recorded the curious cornucopia-flanked dome at Front and Market Streets. Photographers of the 1850s and 1860s projected a fragile sense of history in their images of old and threatened places. Only three of the 11 buildings pictured in this group of photographs survived into the twentieth century: Independence Hall, Carpenters' Hall and the now altered and forgotten Christ Church Hospital.

Richards and his short-time partner John Betts knew that the Chestnut Street Theatre would not outlast the dedication of the Academy of Music on Broad Street. Impending destruction also motivated Richards to photograph the Falstaff Hotel. The tavern near the Chestnut Street Theatre was remembered for its owner in the 1830s, theatrical entrepreneur William Warren, who appeared on its painted sign as the jovial character Falstaff with the words, "Shall I not take mine ease in mine inn?" With a mind to such facts, the antiquarians Charles A. Poulson, Jr. and John McAllister, Jr. purchased these photographs from their makers, and guided them to additional sites. This spirit is embodied in images of the Bell Tavern, a watering place for eighteenth-century politicians; the Old London Coffee House, a busy center of pre-Revolutionary activity; Carpenters' Hall; and Independence Hall.

In the 1860s, photographers went further afield in pursuit of forgotten places of history. John Moran, the quintessential antiquarian photographer, crossed the Schuylkill River in June 1867 and recorded the Kingsessing School House, then abandoned and covered with graffiti. The photograph attributed to Robert Newell shows another schoolhouse, the survivor of four Northern Liberties market sheds built in 1783. Institutions that had moved to larger facilities, leaving behind empty buildings, such as the 1819 Christ Church Hospital on Cherry Street, were also considered endangered and were photographed.

DOMESTIC
(Illustrations 81–86)

A good portion of Philadelphia's mid-century soul thrived in the libraries of two busy men: John Jay Smith and Ferdinand J. Dreer. Smith was an historian, editor, publisher and horticulturalist, a founder of Laurel Hill Cemetery and librarian of the Library Company. He died at his Germantown estate Ivy Cottage

in 1881. Dreer moved to 1520 Spruce Street after parting with Sedgeley in 1857; the Schuylkill tract was then assimilated into Fairmount Park. The jeweler and autograph collector soon retired to pursue his antiquarian interests for the next four decades.

The railroad suburbs of Philadelphia were an attractive setting for the commodious estates of those with new-found fortunes. The brownstone house of the family of Tradesmen's Bank President Charles H. Rogers on York Road was one of many built during the 1840s. Diarist Sydney George Fisher was impressed with the estate of Rogers, among others, and wrote in 1857: "The railroad and the taste for villa life have done it all, & so manifold are its advantages that the wonder to me is how any can bear to stay in town." These, and dozens of other villas, such as the Italianate residence of painter Samuel Bell Waugh, were photographed by John Moran in the early 1860s.

CHURCHES
(Illustrations 87–90)

The thirteenth-century English country church was imported to Philadelphia in the 1846 designs for St. James the Less. London architect G. G. Place forwarded church-approved drawings based on St. Michael's Church at Long Stanton, Cambridgeshire, to Philadelphia's John E. Carver for the rural site north of the city. St. James's arrangement of vestry, chancel and nave, gem-like in McClees's 1855 photograph, was an architectural definition of current Episcopalian conservatism. Less wealthy churches, such as the unidentified one photographed about 1870, were also influenced by the Gothic revival, though less profoundly. Philadelphia churches of other sects, such as Joseph C. Hoxie's Fourth Baptist Church of 1853, found inspiration in London City churches of the seventeenth century. In the following decades, standard building forms appeared in ever-changing fashionable modes. John Notman's St. Clement's, for instance, built at Twentieth and Cherry Streets in 1859, was eclectically "dressed" in the Romanesque manner.

GOVERNMENT BUILDINGS
(Illustrations 91–97)

When Charles Dickens visited Philadelphia in 1841, he noted the "mournful, ghost-like aspect" of the empty Second Bank of the United States, symbol of the political battle won by President Andrew Jackson five years before. By the time of Robert Newell's photograph in the late 1860s, the Doric temple on Chestnut Street had become the United States Custom House, a function it served into the 1930s. Its architect, William Strickland, also designed the United States Mint at Chestnut and Juniper Streets, another symbol of national monetary strength. The Mint opened in 1833, six years before Joseph Saxton made Philadelphia's first daguerreotypes from its windows.

Government buildings projected social messages as well. In 1823, the Commonwealth hired John Haviland to design the Eastern State Penitentiary, an immense castellated Gothic pile on Fairmount Avenue between Twentieth and Twenty-second Streets. The Quaker-inspired reform theory of solitary confinement was introduced within its walls, giving this prison international fame. McClees photographed this still-extant tribute to American masonry in 1858.

A progressive step toward the monumentality of City Hall, Philadelphia's most notable example of grandiose municipal architecture, was the 1848 Spring Garden Hall, also photographed by McClees. The eclectic design of its steeple, probably influenced by the contemporary Smithsonian Institution competition, appears strident in combination with a standard classical facade.

Having no traditional architectural language of its own, industry adopted forms originally developed for other purposes. The Retort House of the Point Breeze Gas Works was built in 1859 by John C. Cresson, who utilized the space-making solution of Gothic Revival church builders: a high iron-vaulted nave on shorter masonry walls. The engineer's son, Charles M. Cresson, photographed the building soon after it opened. Upstream on the Schuylkill were the classical and picturesque waterworks at Fairmount, Philadelphia's major water source from 1822 until the city's consolidation in 1854. At that time the 24th Ward Water Works was built even further up the Schuylkill to provide for West Philadelphia. The curious dome of its engine house, part of the design by the firm of Birkinbine and Trotter, was doubtlessly inspired by Philadelphia's first waterworks at Center Square, a design itself arbitrarily borrowed from Classical Revival funerary architecture.

INSTITUTIONS
(Illustrations 98–103)

On May 28, 1855, the *Public Ledger* reported: "J. E. McClees, the Photographer, is producing some admirable photographs of the public buildings of Philadelphia." The finest is a print of Jefferson Medical College, a Tenth Street institution enlarged with a classical facade a decade earlier by architect Napoleon Le Brun. McClees's luxurious print heralded the rise in paper photography; by the early 1860s hundreds of stereographs of public buildings were published by the firm of McAllister and Brother. In 1860, John A. McAllister accelerated the search for pictorial material in a letter to architect Thomas U. Walter requesting a list of "all the public buildings" he erected. Walter responded with a list of 50, many of which soon appeared in stereographs. Few of these pictures were superior to those of the Langenheim brothers, who photographed the recently finished interior of the new Masonic Hall on Chestnut Street. This extravagant interior of the American Gothic Revival, designed by

Edward Collins and C. M. Autenrieth, is known today by an 1855 chromolithograph by Max Rosenthal. The Langenheims' photograph is far truer.

Collins and Autenrieth lost an architectural competition to Frank Furness in 1879 for the Locust and Juniper Street building of The Library Company of Philadelphia. The new library, photographed in 1880, was designed to bear a skeletal resemblance to its Fifth Street predecessor. Its neighborhood, Broad Street South, was fast becoming an avenue of halls, clubs, churches and hotels. In 1855, a photograph was made of part of its growth: the Sansom Street Academy of Natural Sciences, an early commission of John Notman, and the recently completed La Pierre House by John McArthur, Jr. A decade later, the patriotic gentlemen's Union League opened on the opposite side of Sansom Street. As Philadelphia's growth moved the center of business and culture west up Chestnut Street, and then onto Broad, institutions in the eastern part of the city, such as the 1834 Merchants' Exchange at Third and Dock Streets, languished.

BUSINESS AND INDUSTRY
(Illustrations 104–117)

When the Public Ledger building opened at Sixth and Chestnut Streets in 1867, Edwin T. Freedley, a writer on manufactures, called it "the most extensive and splendid building for printing purposes in the United States." The twopenny *Ledger* was the most popular of a dozen Philadelphia daily newspapers, with a circulation comparable to that of the *London Standard*. In this new building designed by John McArthur, Jr. and photographed by Frederick Gutekunst, we find a familiar expression of the power of the press.

The *Ledger's* first issue had been printed at the Philadelphia Arcade in 1836. In Richards' 1859 photograph of the Arcade Hotel, the original building designed by John Haviland is pierced with bulk windows and partially obscured by a cast-iron balcony. The original marble mall of 1827 contained 80 shops along two skylighted aisles stretching from the Chestnut Street entrances. Later the Arcade housed the Peale Museum and a commodious public bath. After alterations in the late 1850s it opened once again as the Arcade Hotel. This final attempt at financial stability soon ended in bankruptcy, after the new and much larger Continental Hotel, just a few blocks to the west at Ninth Street, proved a greater attraction to the nation's visiting social and business elite.

The tastes of wealthy Philadelphians of the mid-century were served by retailers throughout the city, such as the glass and china store of Wanner, Kline & Co. on North Third Street, but more especially by the exclusive purveyors along Chestnut Street. Opposite the Arcade, at 718, was the chandelier showroom of Warner, Miskey & Merrill, a firm whose artistic reputation led to a commission for the menagerie-laden bronze stair rails in the newly remodeled chambers of the

House and Senate in Washington. Paintings by native and expatriate American artists were purchased on the next block at James S. Earle & Son's. Still further up Chestnut Street in a new ornamental building adjacent to the Continental Hotel was Bailey & Co., considered nationally the finest jewelers and silversmiths. "Warner, Miskey & Merrill's Show Room" and "Bailey & Co's Jewelry Store," both Langenheim stereographs of 1860, were backed with printed advertisements and used as business cards.

The most popular photographers—M. A. Root, Frederick and William Langenheim, David C. Collins, Samuel Broadbent, Montgomery P. Simons and a score of others—had Chestnut Street studios. In 1853, McClees and Germon made a print depicting the daguerrean practice at their second-floor salon on Chestnut Street between Seventh and Eighth. The stereograph proved paper photography a worthwhile enterprise in the busy shop of McAllister and Brother at 728. And by the late 1860s, the walls in the establishment of Wenderoth, Taylor & Brown, 914 Chestnut Street, formerly the studio of daguerrean Samuel Broadbent, were covered with framed prints.

Industry thrived on the city's periphery; John and Matthew Baird had sawn and prepared marble at their Spring Garden Street works since the 1840s. By the 1870s John Baird had moved the establishment to a Schuylkill site. John Moran photographed their earlier works. The I. P. Morris & Company engine factory on the Delaware at Port Richmond was photographed in 1860. Engines for the United States Mint were built at this works from its beginning in 1846. After a boiler explosion in 1861 (see Ill. 159) and immediate reconstruction, I. P. Morris & Company made engines for the double-turreted ironclad ships in the Civil War and heavy machinery for industries throughout the Union.

54. "William Penn's Mansion, or the 'Slate-roof house.'—South-east cor. of Norris alley, and Second street." Salt print by Frederick DeBourg Richards, August 1854.

55. "Loxley House. Cor. (S.E.) little Dock and Second street." Salt print by
Frederick DeBourg Richards and [John] Betts, January 1854.

56. ''Chew's Mansion, Germantown.'' Albumen print by James E. McClees,
February 1857.

57. "Old wooden houses, extending southwardly from the corner of Marble street, on the westside of Tenth street." Salt print by Frederick DeBourg Richards, March 1859.

58. Burd Mansion, Chestnut Street at Ninth, southwest corner. Albumen print by an unidentified photographer, ca. 1860.

59. "Jefferson House. So. west corner of Seventh and Market St." Salt print by
James E. McClees, 1855.

60. "Birthplace of Benjamin West 1869." Albumen print by John Moran.

61. "House in Mickle's Court 1869." Albumen print by John Moran.

62. "Christian St above Front 1868." Platinum print from negative by John Moran, ca. 1890.

63. "Winfield Place." Albumen print by John Moran, ca. 1869.

64. "Little Dock & Spruce." Albumen print attributed to Henry B. Odiorne,
March 1860.

TOP: **65.** "Old building NE Cor 32nd & Chestnut (Keen Residence)." From a negative by John C. Browne, March 27, 1882. BOTTOM: **66.** "Trent House. 13th St. bel. Passyunk Avenue Philada. built 1700 to 1709." From a negative by John C. Browne, November 1885.

TOP: **67.** "Old House 18th & Diamond Sts. [Kohn mansion]." From a negative by John C. Browne, January 4, 1882. BOTTOM: **68.** "Old Spring House Mill Creek Mont. Co. Pa." Platinum print attributed to John C. Browne, 1882.

69. "Dr. Staughton's, or Sansom St. Baptist Church. Sansom, So. side E. of Ninth Street." Salt print by Frederick DeBourg Richards, March 1858.

70. "Stereoscopic View of a Portion of Market Street, Philadelphia, Looking West, embracing the Cupola of the Market House." Albumen print by Henry B. Odiorne, 1859.

71. "Chestnut Street Theatre." Chestnut Street, between Sixth and Seventh, north side. Salt print by Frederick DeBourg Richards and [John] Betts, 1854.

72. Falstaff Hotel. "Northwest corner of Carpenter and Sixth Street, North of Chestnut Street." Salt print by Frederick DeBourg Richards, June 1857.

73. ''Bell Tavern—West side of Eighth Street North of Sansom Street (A primitive building).'' Salt print by Frederick DeBourg Richards, May 1857.

74. "Old London coffee-House. S.W. corner of Market and Front Street." Salt
print by James E. McClees, August 1858.

75. "Carpenters' Court, and Hall, (in perspective) Chestnut st. bet. Third &
Fourth st." Salt print by Frederick DeBourg Richards, May 1859.

76. "Independence Hall or State House From the N.E. across the ruins made by the great fire. N.W. corner of Chestnut and Fifth St." Salt print by James E. McClees, spring of 1856.

77. ''Vestibule of Independence Hall—1869.'' Albumen print by John Moran.

78. "Kingsessing School House—June 1867." Albumen print by John Moran.

79. Callowhill and New Market Streets. Albumen print attributed to Robert Newell, ca. 1868.

80. Christ Church Hospital, 306–308 Cherry Street. Albumen print attributed to
John Moran, ca. 1867.

TOP: **81.** "Interior of Library of F. J. Dreer Esq. Philada." Albumen-print stereograph by John Moran, 1864. BOTTOM: **82.** "Mr. Dreer's Library, Phila." Albumen-print stereograph by John Moran, 1864.

TOP: **83.** ''Library in Ivy Cottage.'' Estate of John Jay Smith, Germantown. Albumen print by an unidentified photographer, ca. 1875. BOTTOM: **84.** ''Villas, Near Philadelphia, Estate of C. H. Rogers.'' Albumen-print stereograph by John Moran, 1864.

TOP: **85.** "Views on the Estate of S. B. Waugh, Bordentown, N. J." Albumen-print stereograph by John Moran, ca. 1864. BOTTOM: **86.** "Residence of S. B. Waugh, Artist, at Bordentown, N. J." Albumen-print stereograph by John Moran, ca. 1864.

87. "Church of St. James the Less (Episcopal)." Clearfield and Thirty-second
Streets. Salt print by James E. McClees, 1855.

88. Church Interior. Albumen print, unidentified photographer, ca. 1870.

89. ''Baptist Church 5th & Buttonwood Sts. July 1858.'' Albumen print by James E. McClees.

90. St. Clement's Episcopal Church from the Southwest, Twentieth and Cherry Streets. Albumen print attributed to John Moran, ca. 1863.

91. Custom House, Chestnut Street between Fourth and Fifth, south side. Albumen print attributed to Robert Newell, ca. 1868.

92. The United States Mint, northwest corner of Chestnut and Juniper Streets.
Salt print attributed to James E. McClees, 1855.

93. Eastern State Penitentiary, Fairmount Avenue between Twentieth and Twenty-second Streets. Albumen print attributed to James E. McClees, ca. 1858.

94. ''Spring Garden Hall. N.W. Corner of Thirteenth & Spring Garden St.'' Salt print by James E. McClees, 1855.

95. "Retort House of Point Breeze gas works. John C. Cresson engineer." Salt print by Charles M. Cresson, ca. 1860.

96. Waterworks. "Fairmount Park, Philadelphia." Albumen print by James Cremer, 1876.

97. "Engine House of the Twenty-Fourth Ward Water Works. Designed and Constructed by Birkinbine and Trotter, Engineers and Contractors, Philadelphia." Salt print by an unidentified photographer, ca. 1854.

98. "Jefferson Medical college. So. Tenth Street." Salt print by James E. McClees, 1855.

99. "The Library Co. of Philadelphia N.W. cor Locust & Juniper St. opened
Feb. 24, 1880." Albumen print by an unidentified photographer, ca. 1880.

100. Academy of Natural Sciences and La Pierre House, Broad and Sansom Streets, northwest corner. Salt print attributed to James E. McClees, ca. 1855.

TOP: **101.** "Grand Lodge Room, New Masonic Hall, Philadelphia." Albumen-print stereograph by William and Frederick Langenheim, ca. 1860. BOTTOM: **102.** "Smoking Room, Philada. Union League." Albumen-print stereograph by an unidentified photographer, ca. 1867.

103. Merchants' Exchange, Dock Street at Walnut. Albumen print by an unidentified photographer, ca. 1865.

104. "Public Ledger Building, S. W. Corner Sixth and Chestnut Streets, Philadelphia. Opened June 20, 1867." Albumen print by Frederick Gutekunst, 1867.

105. Arcade Hotel. ''North side of Chestnut street, west of Sixth Street.'' Salt print by Frederick DeBourg Richards, January 1858.

106. Strangers Guide Book Stand, Continental Hotel Lobby. Ninth and Chestnut Streets. Unmounted salt-print stereograph by an unidentified photographer, ca. 1860.

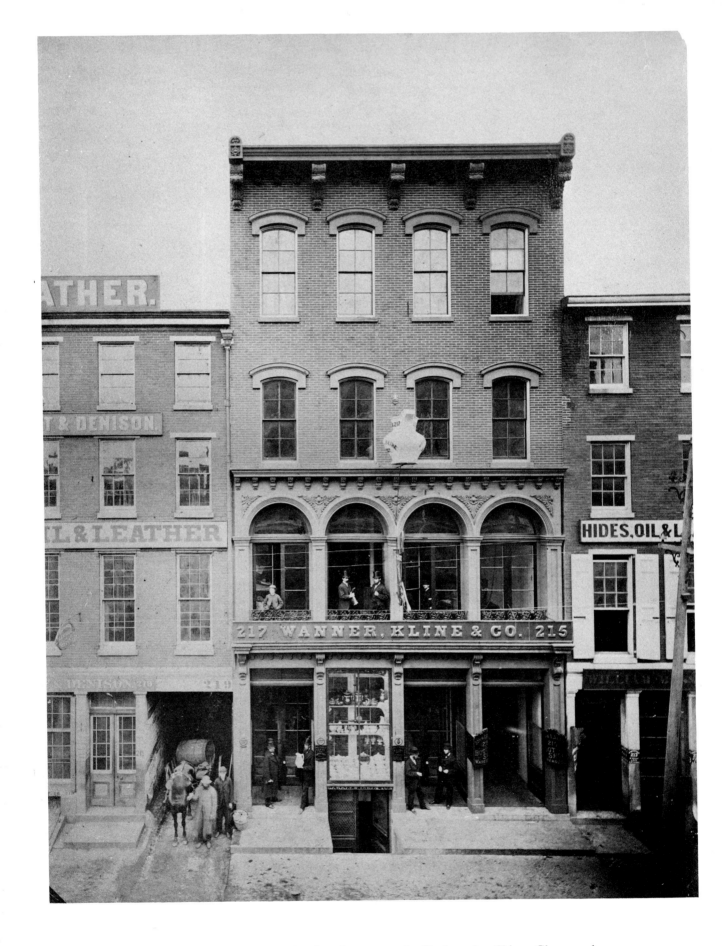

107. "Wanner, Kline & Co. Importers & Dealers in China Glass and Queensware. Nos. 215 & 217 North Third Street." Albumen print attributed to Frederick A. Wenderoth, ca. 1868.

108. Market Street Commercial Establishments. Albumen print by an unidentified photographer, ca. 1868.

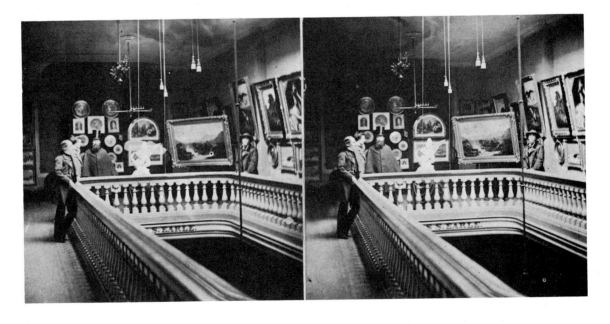

TOP: **109.** "Warner Miskey & Merrill's Show Room, 718 Chestnut St. Phil."
Albumen-print stereograph by William and Frederick Langenheim, ca. 1860.
BOTTOM: **110.** Interior of James S. Earle & Son, 816 Chestnut Street. Albumen-
print stereograph attributed to John Moran, ca. 1861.

TOP: **111.** "Bailey & Co's Jewelry Store, 918 Chestnut St., Philad'a." Albumen-print stereograph by William and Frederick Langenheim, ca. 1860. BOTTOM: **112.** "McAllister & Brother, 728 Chestnut Street, Philadelphia." Albumen-print stereograph attributed to John Moran, ca. 1861.

113. McClees & Germon Daguerreotype Rooms, Chestnut Street between Seventh and Eighth, south side. Salt print attributed to James E. McClees, 1853.

TOP: **114.** "Wenderoth, Taylor & Brown, Fine Art Gallery, No. 914 Chestnut St., Philadelphia." Albumen-print stereograph by Wenderoth, Taylor & Brown, ca. 1869. BOTTOM: **115.** I. P. Morris & Company Iron Works, Port Richmond, Philadelphia. Albumen-print stereograph attributed to Frederic Graff, ca. 1860.

TOP: **116.** John and Matthew Baird, Marble Works, Spring Garden Street above Ridge Road. Albumen print attributed to John Moran, ca. 1864. BOTTOM: **117.** "Warerooms of Baird's Monumental Works." Albumen-print stereograph attributed to John Moran, ca. 1864.

OBJECTS

ANTIQUARIAN
(Illustrations 118–128)

Nineteenth-century antiquarians cultivated a hearty brand of historicism. From bits and pieces of the past they composed a rich texture of associations, giving old Philadelphia a familiarity in the midst of vast new growth. Photography sharpened the edge of fleeting time and was used to represent history-laden objects such as the front door of Cliveden ("Chew House"), the parlor hearth at Graeme Park and the steeple of Christ Church. Sentimental treasures of the mid-century, William Penn's wampum belt from his treaty with the Indians and the Liberty Bell in Independence Hall, were often photographed. As the century wore on, antiquarian lustre was shed upon newer objects such as the *Nymph and Bittern* fountain originally sculptured in 1809 by William Rush for Center Square.

Antiquarians had photographic copies made of daguerreotypes, paintings, drawings and printed matter of historical interest. A daguerrotype of Charles Gilpin made during his term as mayor in the early 1850s was reproduced before the decade's end, and an 1855 daguerreotype of Rembrandt Peale was copied after the artist's death five years later. Composite photographs wove a wealth of historical associations into a single image, but the essence of antiquarianism was in the presentation of the rarest objects. For example, a Christmas broadside of 1773 printed by William and Thomas Bradford for newsboys to distribute in return for tips was photographed by McClees for the collector Charles Poulson in the mid-1850s; no copy of the original has been located.

INDUSTRIAL
(Illustrations 129–136)

Pictures generate familiarity. The large colored lithographs of the 1840s popularized new engines, but only the illusion of photography could make the productions of American industry a hand-held reality. McClees's striking portrait of Joseph C. Gartley's portable steam engine, for example, photographed outside the shop where it was built in August 1858, reflects a naïve pride and respect. By 1871, Baldwin Locomotive works catalogues were illustrated with photographs of the engines as they emerged from the factory onto North Broad Street. Although we find McClees's picture the more appealing, his sentiments had no place in the in-dustrial imperative. Mass-produced stereographs and cartes-de-visite also aimed at little more than the representation of a polished engine. The famous Wecaccoe hand pump, an 1840s design by John Agnew, and the 1857 Philadelphia Hose Company "steamer," which made hand pumps obsolete, were both photographed in the early 1860s.

Industry found in photography a public-relations tool. In 1854, the new screw-cutting machine at Morris, Tasker & Morris, Philadelphia pipemakers, was demonstrated before the camera of William and Frederick Langenheim. Joseph Harrison, Jr.'s explosion-proof steam boiler was photographed during installation at the machine-tool manufactory of William Sellers & Company in 1859. A copy of the photograph appeared as the frontispiece in an account of the boiler's reliability published eight years later, quite a contrast to the 1858 composition of a crane at the marble yard of J. Struthers and Son. And photographs of industrial exhibits at the Great Central Fair in 1864, and again at the Centennial, further fixed industry's image in the public mind.

FOUNTAINS, MONUMENTS AND STATUARY
(Illustrations 137–146)

Monumental things that adorn cities lose much of their impact in photographs. By contrast with portraiture, mirror-like and complex, cold stone photographed is profoundly simple. A fountain at the intersection of paths in a park, or one in a private garden or along a creek road is an object experienced during an afternoon walk. Statues hidden along the densest trails, such as the 1902 limestone *Tedyuscung,* an eighteenth-century Delaware Indian chief, were intended to be lore-laden discoveries. Tombs and monuments in stylish suburban cemeteries were designed to compete for Victorian pathos. Out of their contexts and in photographs, these objects become symbols of the life in which they had a part.

CITY
(Illustrations 147–156)

Bits of Philadelphia, when photographed, composed a visual equivalent to laudatory prose about the city experience. Ships at the Delaware port attracted the attention of the Langenheims as they might attract our own. Their view of the harbor and other sites—the newly built Chestnut Street bridge over the Schuylkill, a flag snapping in the wind above the Pennsylvania Academy of Fine Arts, an observatory tower on the Centennial grounds, ornate and monumental entrance-ways, displays of produce at an open market and caged animals in the recently opened Zoological Gardens—compose an impressionistic view of the city. Unlike the formal views of public buildings and historic sites, these images imply experience; they demand a viewer's sympathy. From them, as from a poem or a film, is formulated what Philadelphia was like.

118. Chew House Entrance. Albumen print by an unidentified photographer, ca. 1867.

119. "Interior of Graham [Graeme] Park House   September 1869." Albumen print by John Moran.

TOP: **120.** Christ Church Steeple. Albumen-print stereograph attributed to John Moran, published by McAllister and Brother, ca. 1860. BOTTOM: **121.** Artifacts in the Historical Society of Pennsylvania. Albumen print attributed to John C. Browne, ca. 1868.

122. Liberty Bell in Independence Hall. Albumen-print stereograph by John Moran, ca. 1865.

123. Waterwheel, Platinum print attributed to John C. Browne, ca. 1882.

124. Nymph and Bittern at Fairmount. Gelatine print by William Nicholson Jennings, ca. 1895.

125. Daguerreotype of Charles Gilpin (1809–1891). Salt print by an unidentified
photographer, ca. 1860.

126. Daguerreotype of Rembrandt Peale (1778–1860) by Samuel Root, 1855. Salt print attributed to James E. McClees, 1860.

127. Composite Portrait of American Statesmen. Albumen print by an unidentified photographer, ca. 1865.

Chriſtmas-Box

FOR THE CUSTOMERS OF THE

PENNSYLVANIA JOURNAL.

FRIDAY Afternoon 5 o'Clock, Dec. 24, 1773.

PHILADELPHIA, Dec. 24.

A Two o'Clock this Afternoon arrived in this City a Gentleman, who came Expreſs from New-York, with the following intereſting Advices from BOSTON, which were ſent there by Expreſs also.

BOSTON, DEC. 16.

IT being underſtood that Mr. Rotch, owner of the ſhip Dartmouth, rather lingered in his preparations to return her to London, with the Eaſt-India Company's Tea on board, there was on Monday laſt, P. M. a meeting of the Committee of ſeveral of the neighbouring towns, in Boſton, and Mr. Rotch was ſent for, an enquired of whether he continued his reſolution to comply with the injunctions of the body aſſembled, at the Old-South Meeting-Houſe, on Monday and Tueſday preceeding. Mr. Rotch anſwered, that in the interim he had taken the advice of the beſt council, and found that in caſe he went on of his own motion, to ſend that ſhip to ſea in the condition, ſhe was then in, .. muſt ievitably ruin him, and therefore h muſt beg them to conſider what he had ſaid at the ſaid meeting, to be the effect of compulſion and unadviſed, and in conſequence that he w not holden to abide by it, when he was now aſſured that he muſt be utterly ruined in caſe he did.

Mr. Rotch was then aſked whether he would demand a clearance for his ſhip in the Cuſtom-Houſe, and in caſe of a refuſal enter protest, and then apply in like manner for a paſs, and order her to ſea. To all which he anſwered in the negative, the committees, doubtleſs, informing their reſpective conſtituents of what had paſſed, a very full meeting of the body was again aſſembled at the Old-South Meeting-Houſe on Tueſday afternoon, and Mr Rotch being again preſent, was enquired of as before, and a motion was made and ſeconded, that Mr. Rotch be enjoined forthwith to repair to the Collector of the Cuſtoms and demand a clearance for his ſhip, and ten gentlemen were appointed to accompany him as witneſſes of the demand. Mr. Rotch then proceeded with the committee to Mr. Harriſon's lodgings, and made the demand. Mr. Harriſon obſerved, he could not give anſwer till he conſulted the Comptroller, but would at office hours, next morning, give a deciſive anſwer. On the return of Mr. Rotch and the Committee to the Body with this report, the meeting was adjourned to Thurſday morning at ten o'clock.

THURSDAY.

Having met on Thurſday morning, 10 o'clock, they ſent for Mr. Rotch, and aſked him if he had been to the Collector, and demanded a clearance, he ſaid he had; but the Collector ſaid, that he could not, conſiſtent with his duty, give him a clearance, till all the dutiable articles, were out of his ſhip; they then demanded of him whether he had proteſted againſt the Collector; he ſaid he had not: They ordered him upon his peril, to give immediate orders to the Captain, to get his ſhip ready for ſea, that day, enter a proteſt immediately againſt the Cuſtom-Houſe, and then proceed directly to the Governor, (who was at his ſeat at Milton, ſeven miles off) and demand a paſs for his ſhip to go by the Caſtle. They then adjourned to 3 o'clock P. M. to wait on Mr Rotch's return, having met according to adjournment, there was the fulleſt meeting ever known, (it was reckoned, that there were two thouſand men from the country) they waited very patiently till about 5 o'clock, when they found Mr. Rotch did not return, they began to be very uneaſy, called for a diſſolution of the meeting, and finally obtained a vote for it: But the more moderate part of the meeting fearing what would be the conſequences, begging that they would re-conſider their vote, and wait till Mr. Rotch's return, for this reaſon, that they ought to do every thing in their power to ſend the Tea back, according to their reſolves. They obtained a vote, to remain together one hour longer; in about three quarters of an hour Mr. Rotch returned, his anſwer from the Governor was, that he

By the act, any dutiable goods on board a veſſel after lying 20 days in a harbour becomes liable to the payment of the duties. The people waited till the laſt day, and in a few hours the ſhip, (to ſecure the duties then payable) was to have been delivered to the cuſtody of the man of war.

could not give a paſs till the ſhip was cleared by the Cuſtom Houſe, the people immediately, as with one voice, called for a diſſolution, which having obtained, they repaired to Ciffin's wharf, where the tea veſſels lay, proceeded to fix tackles, and hoiſted the tea upon deck; cut the cheſts to pieces, and threw over the ſide; (there ware two ſhips and a brig, Capt. Hall, Bruce, and Coffin, each veſſel having 114 cheſts of tea on board,) they began upon the two ſhips firſt, as they had nothing on board but the tea, then proceeded to the brig, which had hawled to the wharf, but the day before and had but a ſmall part of her cargo out. The Captain of the brig begged they would not begin with his veſſel, as the tea was covered with goods, belonging to different merchants in town, then told him the tea they wanted, and the tea they would have; but if he would go into his cabin quietly, not one article of his goods ſhould be hurt. They immediately proceeded to remove the goods, and then to diſpoſe of the tea.

It was expected that the men of war would have interfered, as all the Captains and other Officers were ordered on board their ſhips before night; and the day before, there were ſix dozen of lanterns ſent on board the Admiral's ſhip. The King-Fiſher, and ſeveral armed ſchooners were rigged and fitted for ſea, and the Gaſpee armed brig, arrived that day from Rhode-Iſland, But the people were determined. It is to be obſerved, that they were extremely careful, that not any of the tea ſhould be ſtolen, ſo kept a good look out, and detected one man filling his pockets, whom they treated very roughly, by tearing his coat off his back, and driving him up the wharf, through thouſands of people, who cuff'd and kicked im as he paſs'd.

We are poſitively informed, that the patriotic inhabitants of Lexington at a late meeting, unanimouſly reſolved againſt the uſe of bohea tea of all ſorts, Dutch or Engliſh importation; and to maniſeſt the ſincerity of their reſolution, they brought together every ounce contained in the town, and committed it to one common bonfire.

We are alſo informed, Charleſtown is in motion to follow the illuſtrious example.

Quere. Would it not materially affect the bringing this deteſtable herb into diſuſe, if every town would enjoin their Select men to deny licences to all houſes of entertainment, who were known to afford tea to their gueſts?

Our reaſon for ſuggeſting this, is the difficulty theſe people are under to avoid diſhing out this poiſon, without ſuch a proviſion in their favour.

We have this moment received intelligence that Mr. Clarke's brigantine, commanded by Captain Loring, bilged at the back of Cape-Cod. The Captain has not landed his Tea there, of which he has 58 cheſts on board, belonging to the Eaſt-India Company.

NEW-YORK, DEC. 22.

Laſt night an expreſs arrived here from Boſton, who left it on Friday laſt, and brings ſundry letters among which is the following, viz.

Boſton, 17th December, 1773.

GENTLEMEN,

YESTERDAY we had a greater Meeting of the Body than ever. The country coming in from twenty miles round, and every ſtep was taken that was practicable for returning the Teas. The moment it was known out of doors, that Mr. Rotch, could not obtain a paſs for his ſhip, by the caſtle, a number of people huzzaed in the ſtreet, and in a very little time, every ounce of the Teas on board of Capts. Hall, Bruce, and Coffin, was immerſed in the Bay, without the leaſt injury to private property.

The ſpirit of the people on this occaſion ſurpriſed all parties, who viewed the ſcene.

We conceived it our duty to afford you the moſt early advice of this intereſting event, by expreſs, which, departing immediately, obliges us to conclude.

By Order of the Committee.

P. S. The other veſſel, viz. Captain Loring, belonging to Meſſrs. Clark, with fifty-eight cheſts, was, by the Act of God, caſt on ſhore, on the back of Cape Cod.

128. Christmas-Box. Salt print by James E. McClees, ca. 1855.

129. "Gartley's portable steam engine. Front ab. Arch August 1858." Albumen print by James E. McClees.

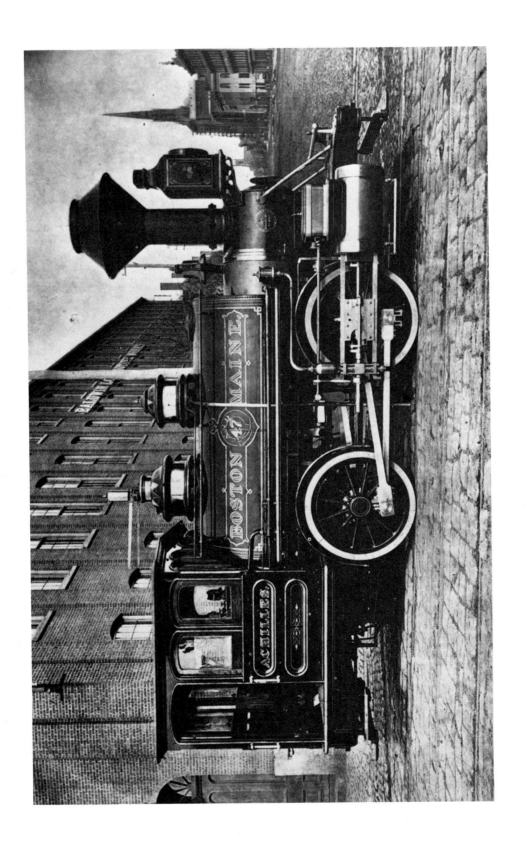

130. Baldwin Locomotive. Carbon print by an unidentified photographer in *Illustrated Catalogue of Locomotives* (Philadelphia: J. B. Lippincott & Co., 1871).

TOP: 131. Philadelphia Hose Company. Albumen-print stereograph by an unidentified photographer, ca. 1863. BOTTOM: 132. Wecaccoe Hand Pump. Albumen-print carte-de-visite by an unidentified photographer, ca. 1864.

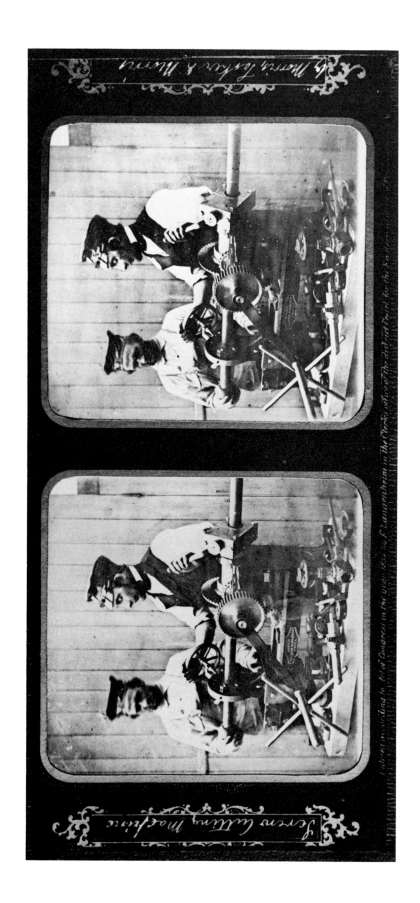

133. "Screw Cutting Machine by Morris, Tasker & Morris." Glass stereograph by William and Frederick Langenheim, 1854.

THE FIRST HARRISON BOILER.

MADE AND PUT IN OPERATION IN THE SPRING OF 1859, AT THE
ESTABLISHMENT OF MESSRS. WM. SELLERS & CO., PHILADELPHIA.
See page 52.

VIEW TAKEN FROM THE REAR BEFORE BEING COVERED WITH BRICK
WORK, and showing Double Furnace before grate bars were put in.
The water-line of this boiler is at the termination of the outside
angles—the fire passing down the centre, and on each side to a
smoke chamber underneath.

134. ''The First Harrison Boiler.'' Albumen print by an unidentified
photographer, 1859, in Joseph Harrison, *An Essay on the Steam Boiler*
(Philadelphia: Lippincott & Co., 1867).

135. Marble Yard of J. Struthers and Son. "Chestnut & 22nd Sts. August 1858."
Albumen print attributed to James E. McClees.

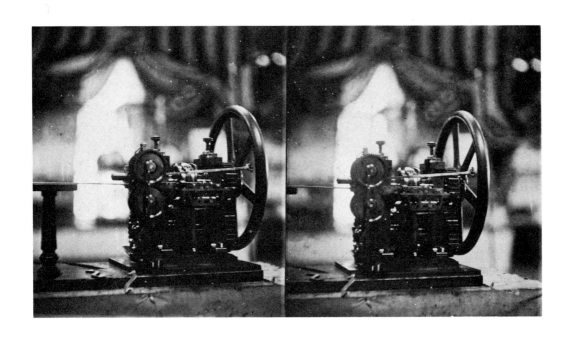

136. ''Horse Shoe Machine, Great Central Fair, Philadelphia, June, 1864.''
Albumen-print stereograph by A. Watson.

137. Fountain. "Fairmount Park, Philadelphia." Albumen print by James Cremer, 1876.

138. "Views in the Garden of J. R. Evans, The Fountain." Albumen-print
stereograph by John Moran, 1864.

139. "Fountain on the Wissahickon put up by Mr. John Cooke." Albumen print
by an unidentified photographer, ca. 1875.

140. ''Figure of the Chief Tedyuscung on the border of the Wissahickon Creek.''
Silver print by an unidentified photographer, ca. 1903.

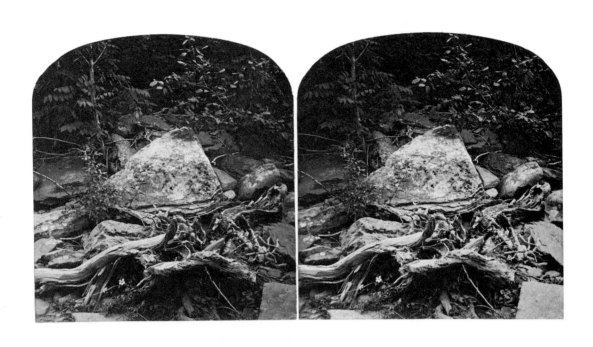

TOP: **141.** "The Hillsides of the Tohicon. Point Pleasant, Bucks County, Pa."
Albumen-print stereograph by John Moran, ca. 1863. BOTTOM: **142.** "F. Graff's
Monument, Fairmount, Phila." Albumen-print stereograph by William and
Frederick Langenheim, ca. 1860.

TOP: **143.** Sepulchral Statue. Albumen-print stereograph attributed to William and Frederick Langenheim, ca. 1860. BOTTOM: **144.** "Tomb Mark W. Collet, M. D. Col. 3rd N. J. Vols. killed at Chancellorville." Saint James the Less, Philadelphia. Albumen-print stereograph by an unidentified photographer, ca. 1864.

145. "Tomb of Aaron Burr," Princeton, New Jersey, with the photographer. Salt print by Frederick DeBourg Richards, September 1854.

146. In the Garden of the Burd Mansion, 9th and Chestnut Street. Albumen-print
stereograph by an unidentified photographer, ca. 1860.

147. "View on the Delaware, Philadelphia Harbor." Albumen-print stereograph by William and Frederick Langenheim, ca. 1860.

TOP: **148.** ''Monitors League Island Philada.'' Albumen-print stereograph by Robert Newell, ca. 1872. BOTTOM: **149.** ''Chestnut St. Bridge Philada.'' Albumen-print stereograph by Bartlett and Smith, ca. 1867.

150. Flag in Front of Pennsylvania Academy of Fine Arts. Albumen print by an unidentified photographer, ca. 1865.

151. ''Observatory, George's Hill Fairmount Park.'' Albumen print by James Cremer, 1876.

152. "Door of Holy Trinity 19th & Walnut St." Albumen-print stereograph
attributed to John Moran, 1859.

153. "Entrance to Woodlands Cemetery Nov. 1858." Albumen print attributed to James E. McClees.

154. Produce. Autochrome by William H. Rau, ca. 1910.

TOP: **155.** Wolf. "Zoological Gardens, Philadelphia. Negatives by Schreiber & Sons . . . James Cremer, Photographer and Publisher." Albumen-print stereograph, 1875. BOTTOM: **156.** Llamas. "Zoological Gardens, Philadelphia. Negatives by Schreiber & Sons . . . James Cremer, Photographer and Publisher." Albumen-print stereograph, 1875.

EVENTS

GENERAL
(Illustrations 157–183)

In depicting events, artists manipulated their subjects as a means of interpretation. Both eighteenth-century history painters and nineteenth-century battlefield photographers contrived scenes in order to summarize entire events in one picture. This license made Benjamin West's *Death of General Wolfe* and Alexander Gardner's "Home of a Rebel Sharpshooter" historical icons rather than mere records of war.

Similarly, the disciplined eye of the mid-century Philadelphia photographer tended toward profound imagery. The few cameramen who ventured out of their studios to photograph celebrations, disasters and dedications intended their representations for posterity. The Langenheims' daguerreotype of an October 1844 Exhibition of American Manufactures in the Chinese Museum building sums up the event without showing exhibits, judges awarding premiums or crowds filling the hall to see the wonders of industrial progress. Intending to capture the essence of the event, the daguerrean composed the scene as he thought it should appear rather than as it actually appeared. Many early photographers chose perspectives rarely experienced in normal vision, summarizing occasions in concise, although unreal images. Often with a less formal approach, photographers emphasized the illusion of presence and involved viewers in the *spirit* of the event. The stereograph of Lincoln's funeral procession, and several of William H. Rau's platinum prints of the Pennsylvania Capitol dedication, captured the essence of the events in spirit alone.

CONSTRUCTION AND DEMOLITION
(Illustrations 184–197)

In the history of American architecture, Benjamin Henry Latrobe's 1798 Classical Revival Bank of Pennsylvania is considered one of the most influential buildings. Latrobe later claimed that "the style of this single building has given to the Philadelphia architecture, even in our plainest brick dwellings, a breadth of effect and a repose vainly sought in other cities." The bank appeared in Birch's engravings, Childs's lithographs and McClees's photographs. It was pulled down in the autumn of 1867, not seven decades after it was completed. As the building neared its demise, John Moran photographed the standing remains. The revival of a millennia-old style could not survive its own century; Moran's image suggests an ironic comparison between the six ionic columns of Pennsylvania marble and the classical ruins of Greece and Rome. For Moran, the bank was as much a part of Philadelphia as the Schuylkill and Delaware Rivers; his photograph expresses disbelief and shock. It is more than a record or a protest; Moran's "Pennsylvania Bank 1867" is one of the most concise and powerful images of mid-century Philadelphia.

Moran's esthetic responsibility and his photographic opportunity to tap public sentiment contributed to the bank print's success. Few of his contemporaries had reason to explore the potential of photography as thoroughly. By comparison, James Cremer's 92 commissioned views of the construction of City Hall are a monthly record of an important though unemotional event. These prints are informative, technically excellent, but uninspired. Cremer did not have the occasion to make them otherwise.

157. Exhibition of the Institute of American Manufactures at the Chinese Museum. Salt print after a daguerreotype by William and Frederick Langenheim, October 1844.

158. "Ruins of Museum Building 9th below Chestnut St. July 1854." Chinese Museum. Salt print by Frederick DeBourg Richards and [John] Betts.

TOP: **159.** "Results of Boiler Explosion of Oct. 19/61." I. P. Morris & Company Iron Works, Port Richmond. Albumen-print stereograph by Frederic Graff. BOTTOM: **160.** "Dr. Jayne's Building Carters alley March 5th 1872." Albumen-print stereograph by William Bell.

161. Hanging of Henry Richards and Alexander Anderson, Lancaster, Pa. April 9, 1858. Salt print by M. H. Locher in *The Manheim Tradgedy* (Lancaster, Pa.: H. A. Rockafield, 1858).

162 & 163. ''Westown Boarding School. Chester Co., Pa.'' Albumen-print cartes-de-visite by John Moran, 1864.

164. ''Regatta at Fairmount.'' Albumen-print stereograph attributed to Robert Newell, ca. 1865.

165. Vendors on Commerce Street at the Opening of the Eastern Market Building. Salt print by an unidentified photographer, November 1859.

166. Ceremonial Dinner at the Opening of the Eastern Market Building. Salt print by an unidentified photographer, November 1859.

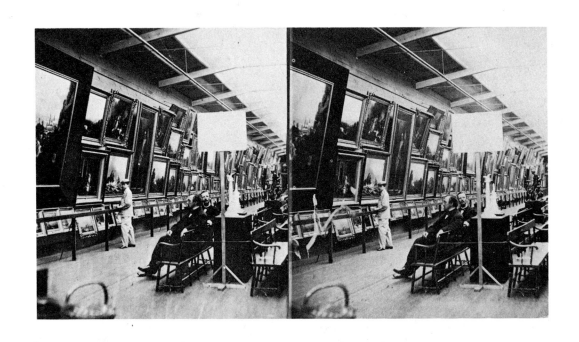

167. ''Fine Art Gallery, Great Central Fair, Philadelphia, June 1864.'' Albumen-print stereograph by A. Watson.

168. ''Union Avenue, Great Central Sanitary Fair, June 1864.'' Albumen print by Robert Newell in *The Philadelphia Photographer,* 1 (October 1864), frontispiece.

169. Pennsylvania Kitchen, Great Central Sanitary Fair, June 1864. Albumen print attributed to Oliver H. Willard.

170. "Centennial Exhibition from Observatory, George's Hill." Albumen print by James Cremer, 1876.

171. Connolly Bros. & McTighe, Automatic Telephone Exchange. International Electrical Exhibition, 1884. Albumen print by an unidentified photographer.

172. Centennial Anniversary of the Lutheran Church, 5th and Cherry Streets.
Albumen-print stereograph by an unidentified photographer, 1866.

173. "7th Presbyterian Church, General Convention 1862." Albumen-print carte-de-visite by an unidentified photographer.

TOP: **174.** "The Funeral of Mr. Lincoln April 22, 1865." Albumen-print stereograph by an unidentified photographer. BOTTOM: **175.** "Chestnut Street from the State House." Albumen-print stereograph by Robert Newell, April 1865.

176. Building of the Supervisory Committee for Recruiting Negro Troops decorated for the Celebration of the Abolition of Slavery in Maryland, November 1864. Albumen print by an unidentified photographer.

177. The Unveiling of the Statue of Benjamin Franklin, Post Office Building. Gelatine print by an unidentified photographer, 1899.

178. The Unveiling of the Statue of Benjamin Franklin, Post Office Building. Gelatine print by an unidentified photographer, 1899.

179. Court of Honor, Peace Jubilee, Broad and Sansom Streets. Gelatine print by William H. Rau, 1898.

180. "Ex. Gov. Stone presenting Capitol to Commonwealth." Platinum print by William H. Rau, Harrisburg, Pa., October 4, 1906.

181. "Pres. Roosevelt making his address." Platinum print by William H. Rau, Harrisburg, Pa., October 4, 1906.

182. "Pres. Roosevelt addressing Crowd." Platinum print by William H. Rau, Harrisburg, Pa., October 4, 1906.

183. "1st Regiment." Platinum print by William H. Rau, Harrisburg, Pa., October 4, 1906.

184. "Pennsylvania Bank 1867." Albumen-print stereograph by John Moran.

185. Demolition of Pennsylvania Bank. Albumen print attributed to John Moran, 1867.

186. ''New City Building, Philadelphia. Views of Construction.'' Albumen-print
stereograph by James Cremer. August 1874.

187. "New City Building, Philadelphia. Views of Construction." Albumen-print stereograph by James Cremer. April 1875.

188. ''New City Building, Philadelphia. Views of Construction.'' Albumen-print
stereograph by James Cremer. August 1875.

189. ''New City Building, Philadelphia. Views of Construction.'' Albumen-print
stereograph by James Cremer. August 1875.

190. "New Pennsylvania Hospital for the Insane, building, Pa." Albumen-print
stereograph by Frederick and William Langenheim, ca. 1859.

LEFT: **191.** Construction of the Cathedral of Saints Peter and Paul. Albumen print attributed to Robert Newell. ca. 1862. RIGHT: **192.** Construction of Holy Trinity Church. Albumen print attributed to John Moran, ca. 1859.

193. Union League and the Academy of Natural Sciences, Broad and Sansom Streets. Albumen print by an unidentified photographer, ca. 1864.

194 & 195. ''Philadelphia Water Works   New Mill House at Fairmount.'' Albumen-print stereographs by H. P. M. Birkinbine, October 1860.

196. Construction at Ninth and Sansom Streets. Albumen-print carte-de-visite by
Broadbent & Co., ca. 1863.

197. Demolition of the Edward Shippen Burd Mansion, 9th and Chestnut Streets.
Albumen print by an unidentified photographer, ca. 1862.

VIEWS

LANDSCAPES
(Illustrations 198–205)

In 1865, Marcus Aurelius Root summarized in *The Camera and the Pencil:* "to represent . . . the beautiful and the sublime in natural scenery; to reproduce . . . the creations of inspired genius; and especially to delineate the human face and figure . . . are to transcribe the matchless pencillings of the Divine Proto-Artist." One year later, John Moran claimed for photography "the ability to create imagery which calls forth ideas and sentiments of the beautiful," agreeing that the viewer's impressions should transcend the immediate reality. Moran and his colleagues trekked through the Pennsylvania hills, long admired for their age and purity, and provided the theories with a practical counterpart.

IMPROVED LANDSCAPES
(Illustrations 206–214)

Richards' antiquarian intent in his prints of Germantown farmhouses, including that of Thomas Godfrey, inventor of an improved mariner's quadrant, had some very landscape-like results. Moran applied his technique of landscape photography to well-known city prospects. McClees's delicate composition of the Schuylkill bank opposite Fairmount was a thematic twist upon the most celebrated of all Philadelphia views. On their way to Niagara in 1854, the Langenheim brothers made views recording the hand of civilization upon rural America. These landscapes describe the coexistence of nature and civilization. By the end of the century, such statements could not be made without a great wash of Pictorialist sentiment.

CITY PANORAMAS
(Illustrations 215–223)

The classic view of eighteenth-century Philadelphia was from the Jersey side of the Delaware River. As the city pushed westward over its two-mile-wide "neck of land," this panorama was replaced by views in series. Prints and photographs of the busiest streets contributed to a spirited nineteenth-century representation of Philadelphia.

Artists strived to find a single panorama for the nineteenth-century city. Views of the Fairmount waterworks, itself an abstraction of the city, often contained a faint skyline in the distance. Prospects from the steeple of Independence Hall, from the roof of Girard College and from imaginary "bird's-eye" vantage points appeared in large mid-century prints. The Langenheim brothers had made a talbotype panorama from Independence Hall in 1849 and dozens of cameramen ascended its steeple during the next several decades. Both the Langenheims and Moran photographed the city from Girard College in the 1860s. Centennial prospects from the new tower at Lemon Hill in Fairmount Park by James Cremer suggested a variety of succinct city views. A few Philadelphians were already fantasizing that a diagonal boulevard connecting the ancient and antithetical sites of Penn Square and Fairmount would make city and park one. Over three decades passed before a building was razed for the Parkway project, which, when complete, provided the standard modern view of Philadelphia.

STREET SCENES
(Illustrations 224–234)

During the first half of the nineteenth century, Philadelphia's character was best captured in picturesque scenes of familiar streets. Hundreds of prints were issued at dedications and celebrations, as advertisements and as commercially published series. The first of these series, 28 engravings by William and Thomas Birch, appeared in 1800. Cephas Grier Childs published 25 lithographic views in 1827–30, and eight years later John Casper Wild offered yet another collection. These and other printmakers had developed pictorial traditions within the constraints of their art and its market. In the 1850s and 1860s, photographers recast these pictorial traditions.

Henry B. Odiorne's masterly street views of 1860 introduced to Philadelphia photography a sophistication not evident in images of the previous decades. Odiorne did not merely record parts of the old city, he employed history to flavor images. These rich albumen prints, and those of John Moran later in the decade, represent an evolution from primitive illustration to pictorial expression. As photographers began to understand the potential of their art, they took on the responsibility of interpretation and with it a perspective that became the basis of modern photographic vision.

198. "Sunset After rain on the Alleghany Mountains." Albumen print attributed
to John Moran, ca. 1865.

199. ''Scenery in the Region of the Delaware Water Gap, Pennsylvania. The Gap, from the Bed of the River.'' Albumen-print stereograph by John Moran and [?] Storey, ca. 1864.

200. River Landscape. From a negative by John C. Browne, ca. 1880.

201. Pennsylvania Landscape. Albumen print attributed to John Moran, ca. 1865.

TOP: **202.** ''At Milestown, near Philadelphia.'' Albumen-print stereograph by John Moran, ca. 1864. BOTTOM: **203.** Creek Scene. Albumen print by John Moran, ca. 1864.

204. ''Fairmount Park, Philadelphia.'' Albumen print by James Cremer, 1876.

205. "Grand Cañon; mouth of Kanab Wash. Colorado River Series." Albumen-
print stereograph by William Bell, 1872.

206. "The house and farm of Godfrey . . . on the corner of Limekiln Road and Church Lane." Salt print by Frederick DeBourg Richards, April 1859.

April 1859 -

207. "Rock House, Shoemakers' lane." Germantown. Salt print by Frederick DeBourg Richards, April 1859.

208. "At Germantown." Albumen print by John Moran, ca. 1865.

209. "Fairmount Waterworks from the [East Side] of the Schuylkill River."
Albumen print by John Moran, ca. 1865.

210. "View of the Toll-House, Superintendent's residence, & part of Schuylkill Canal & c. on the west side of River Schuylkill opposite Fairmount, 1855." Albumen print by James E. McClees.

211. "Mount Carbon from Walker Cottage. Views in the Coal Region near Pottsville, Pa." Glass stereograph by William and Frederick Langenheim, 1854.

212. "R. R. Bridge 230 feet high. Genesee Falls near Portage, N. Y." Glass stereograph by William and Frederick Langenheim, 1854.

213. "Sanc Hollow Track-Tank. Pennsylvania Railroad Scenery." Albumen print by Frederick Gutekunst, ca. 1868.

214. "House Near the Marsh." Platinum print by Clarence B. Moore, ca. 1895.

215. Rooftop View East from 920 Chestnut Street. Albumen print by an
unidentified photographer, ca. 1861.

216. "View of Philadelphia from City Hall looking south. 1894." Print by William H. Rau.

217. "View From Observatory. Lemon Hill. East Fairmount Park." Albumen print by James Cremer, 1876.

218. Girard College and Vicinity. "View From Observatory, Lemon Hill, East Fairmount Park." Albumen print by James Cremer, 1876.

TOP: **219.** ''Philadelphia, from the roof of Girard College.'' Albumen-print stereograph by William and Frederick Langenheim, ca. 1860. BOTTOM: **220.** ''Phila. from Girard College.'' Albumen-print stereograph by John Moran, ca. 1864.

TOP: **221.** Rooftop View of the State House Steeple. Salt print by an unidentified photographer, ca. 1858. BOTTOM: **222.** ''Philadelphia. [West] from State House.'' Albumen-print stereograph by Montgomery P. Simons, ca. 1871.

223. "Scene on the Delaware, Philadelphia." Albumen-print stereograph by
William and Frederick Langenheim, ca. 1860.

224. "Second Street Market, Second and Pine." Albumen-print stereograph by
Montgomery P. Simons, ca. 1871.

225. Market Street at Front. Gelatin print by William Nicholson Jennings, ca. 1905.

226. Chestnut and Strawberry Streets. Sixth-plate daguerreotype by William G. Mason, ca. 1843.

TOP: **227.** "Third Street, above Chestnut." Albumen-print stereograph by Bartlett & French, ca. 1868. BOTTOM: **228.** Chestnut Street from Seventh to Eighth, North Side. Albumen-print stereograph attributed to Henry B. Odiorne, ca. 1859.

229. Chestnut Street in the Snow, East from 920. Albumen print attributed to
Henry B. Odiorne, ca. 1860.

230. "N. W. Corner 4th & Pine." Albumen print attributed to Henry B. Odiorne,
August 1860.

231. "S. E. Corner of South and 2nd." Albumen print by Henry B. Odiorne,
May 1860.

232. ''Nos. 114 & 116 N. Water St. 1868.'' Albumen print by John Moran.

233. Wood & Perot Foundry, 1136 Ridge Road. Albumen print by James E. McClees, ca. 1858.

234. Boathouse Row. Platinum print by William H. Rau, ca. 1895.

SELECTED LIST OF PHOTOGRAPHERS REPRESENTED

BARTLETT & FRENCH (active 1867–69)
George O. Bartlett and William French; city views, stereographs. Bartlett was a commercial photographer in Reading, Pa. by the early 1870s.

BARTLETT & SMITH (active ca. 1867)
George O. Bartlett and [?] Smith; city views, commercial photography.

BELL, WILLIAM (1830–1910; b. England; active 1848–1905)
Daguerrean with James E. McClees and others; exhibited at the Institute of American Manufactures in 1851. Bell was chief photographer of the Army Medical Museum, Washington, D.C., 1865–69, and returned to Philadelphia in 1869 when he purchased McClees's studio. Best known for his work with Lt. George M. Wheeler on the War Department survey west of the 100th meridian in 1872. Active in Philadelphia during the Centennial, and from 1885 in photographic publishing with George Barrie and Sons.

BIRKINBINE, HENRY P. M. (1819–1886)
Amateur photographer; chief engineer of the Philadelphia Water Department, 1859–80.

BROADBENT, SAMUEL (1810–1880; b. Wethersfield, Conn.; active from 1851)
Portrait and miniature painter before learning the daguerrean art from Samuel F. B. Morse. Broadbent worked in the South before 1851. He exhibited at the Institute of American Manufactures in 1851–52 and his Philadelphia studio was known as Broadbent and Company until 1863. After a hiatus of seven years, he worked with H. C. Phillips, 1870-74; then with W. C. Taylor, 1875–79.

BROWNE, JOHN COATS (1838–1918; b. Philadelphia; active from the early 1860s)
Amateur, frequent contributor to *The Philadelphia Photographer*; manager of Episcopal Hospital, collector of minerals, prints and broadsides. Browne wrote the brief *History of the Photographic Society of Philadelphia* in 1884.

CENTENNIAL PHOTOGRAPHIC COMPANY (active ca. 1876)
Founded by Montreal photographer William Notman, who was succeeded by Edward L. Wilson, publisher of *The Philadelphia Photographer*, and W. Irving Adams. Their catalogue lists over 3000 views of the Centennial Exposition offered in five formats: stereograph to 17-by-21-inches.

COLLINS, THOMAS P. AND DAVID C. (active 1844–51)
Daguerreans; portraits and city views. David C. Collins was in partnership with M. A. Root in 1844 and probably with M. P. Simons, 1845–46. Samples of his work were exhibited at the Institute of American Manufactures, 1844–46.

COONLEY AND WOLFERSBERGER (active 1862–63)
J. Frank Coonley and W. A. Wolfersberger, portraiture. Coonley worked for Mathew B. Brady and George M. Barnard during the Civil War.

CORLIES, SAMUEL FISHER (1830–1888; b. Philadelphia; active 1880s)
Amateur photographer, lawyer; member of The Photographic Exchange Club.

CORNELIUS, ROBERT (1809–1893; b. Philadelphia; active 1839–44)
In the spring of 1840, Cornelius opened the city's first daguerrean studio. By 1842 he rejoined his family's more lucrative brass foundry, Cornelius and Baker, best known for ornate gas fixtures and chandeliers.

CREMER, JAMES (1821–1893; b. England; active 1853–81)
Cremer arrived in the United States in 1843. He worked in New York and Boston before selling daguerreotype stock in Philadelphia. In 1856 Cremer exhibited a melanotype (tintype) at the Institute of American Manufactures. He made portraits and was a prolific stereographer.

CRESSON, CHARLES M. (active 1852–64)
Amateur photographer, physician; engineer at the Philadelphia Gas Works.

DINMORE, WALTER (active 1858–61)
Daguerreotype and paper portraiture.

EAKINS, THOMAS (1844–1916; b. Philadelphia; active from 1875)
Painter and teacher; made photographic portraits and studies.

GERMON, WASHINGTON LAFAYETTE (1823–1878; active from 1846)
In 1845, Germon was an engraver of bank notes and business cards. He was in partnership with James E. McClees, 1846–55, making portraits and city views. Their daguerreotypes were exhibited at the Institute of American Manufactures from 1846, in addition to talbotypes in 1851 and crystallotypes in 1853. Germon continued with studio portraiture after 1856, exhibiting his work that year.

GILLIAMS AND STRATTON SYNDICATE (active ca. 1896)
Leslie E. Gilliams and Richard C. Stratton's press syndicate made city views. By 1900, Gilliams was

alone and continued to 1911 with a business including photoengraving.

GODDARD, PAUL BECK (1811–1866; b. Baltimore, Md.; active from 1839)

Physician, chemist. Goddard's 1839 investigations into the daguerreotype process led to his discovery of a bromide accelerator which reduced exposure time and made portraiture feasible.

GOLDENSKY, ELIAS (1868–1943; b. Russia; active from 1897)

Portraiture. Exhibitor at the Philadelphia Photographic Salon of 1898.

GRAFF, FREDERIC (1817–1890; b. Philadelphia; active from 1859)

In 1842, Graff was assistant engineer of the Philadelphia Water Department, where he became chief engineer, continuing there until 1872.

GUTEKUNST, FREDERICK (1831–1917; b. Germantown, Pa.; active after 1856)

Prolific portraitist. Exhibited a sample of penmanship at the Institute of American Manufactures in 1856; exhibited photographs in 1874. Claimed to make the world's largest photograph in 1876, of the Centennial grounds. Purchased the U.S. rights to the phototype in 1878. Exhibited in the 1889 Exhibition of photographs at the Pennsylvania Academy of Fine Arts.

JENNINGS, WILLIAM NICHOLSON (1860–1946; b. England; active from 1880)

Jennings arrived in Philadelphia in 1878, and was an amateur photographer until the early 1890s, when he joined Frederick Eugene Ives with early color. He experimented with aerial and X-ray photography and after 1900 was a commercial photographer.

LANGENHEIM, WILLIAM (1807–1874; b. Germany) AND FREDERICK (1809–1879; b. Germany; active 1843–74)

Daguerreans; innovators with paper photography after purchase of U.S. rights to the talbotype in 1846. Introduced and popularized the stereograph in 1854. Exhibited daguerreotypes at the Institute of American Manufactures, 1844–49; talbotypes, 1849–50. In 1874, Frederick Langenheim exhibited examples of their glass slides.

LEA, MATHEW CAREY (1821–1897; b. Philadelphia; active from 1839)

Pioneering photochemist, author of *A Manual of Photography*, 1858.

McCLEES, JAMES EARLE (1821–1887; b. Chester County, Pa.; active 1844–69)

Learned the daguerrean trade from M. P. Simons, 1844; in partnership with W. L. Germon, 1846–55; worked with paper printing from 1851. McClees and Germon exhibited daguerreotypes at the Institute of American Manufactures between 1846 and 1853 intermittently; talbotypes in 1851 and crystalotypes in 1853. McClees continued as a daguerrean into the late 1850s. After 1869, when he sold his business to William Bell, McClees was a dealer in paintings, frames and mirrors.

MASON, WILLIAM G. (active 1839–43)

Wood engraver; stationer; teacher of drawing, 1822–60. Made daguerreotypes, 1839–43, city views, engravings.

MOORE, CLARENCE BLOOMFIELD (1852–1936; b. Philadelphia; active from 1889)

Paper manufacturer, book collector, amateur archeologist of the American Indian, Moore exhibited at the Pennsylvania Academy of Fine Arts in 1889. He won third prize in an 1894 *American Amateur Photographer* competition after Alfred Clements and Alfred Stieglitz, and was an exhibitor in the Philadelphia Photographic Salon of 1898.

MORAN, JOHN (1831–1903; b. England; active 1859–85)

Arrived in America in 1844. Painter, landscape and city photographer, prolific stereographer. In partnerships making stereographs with [?] Kindler in 1859, [?] Storey in 1864. Expedition photographer with Commodore T. O. Selfridge to the Isthmus of Darien in Panama, 1871, and to Tasmania and South Africa in 1874 with the U.S. team to observe the transit of Venus. Active member of the Photographic Society of Philadelphia, contributor to *The Philadelphia Photographer*.

MUYBRIDGE, EADWEARD (1830–1904; b. England; active from 1867)

Western expeditions; worked in Philadelphia preparing *Animal Locomotion*, Philadelphia, 1887.

NEWELL, ROBERT (active 1856–1903)

Frame maker before 1856, when he exhibited portraits at the Institute of American Manufactures. Stereographs, city views.

ODIORNE, HENRY B. (active 1859–61)

Working from the studio of Isaac Rehn, Odiorne made city views and stereographs.

RAU, WILLIAM HERMAN (1855–1920; b. Philadelphia; active from 1874)

Topographical photography, city views, portraiture. Rau joined the 1874 U.S. expedition to observe the transit of Venus and was employed by the Pennsylvania Railroad and the Lehigh Railroad in the 1890s. He exhibited at the Pennsylvania Academy of Fine Arts in 1889 and 1898.

REHN, ISAAC (active 1845–77)

Painter before becoming photographer; held one-quarter interest in the ambrotype with James A. Cutting of Boston; exhibited ambrotypes at the Institute of American Manufactures in 1856. Involved in photolithography from 1858.

RICHARDS, FREDERICK DEBOURG (1822–1903; b. Wilmington, Del.; active from 1848)

Portraits, city views. Richards exhibited daguerreotypes at the Institute of American Manufactures from 1848 to 1856, except for 1851. He exhibited talbotypes in 1852, crystalotypes in 1855. From 1854 to 1857 Richards was in partnership with [John] Betts. Author of photographically illustrated *Random Sketches, or What I Saw In Europe*, Philadelphia, 1857. After Richards ended his commercial work in photography in 1865, he became a prominent landscape and marine artist, working primarily in etching, watercolors and oils, though continuing to make photographs.

ROOT, MARCUS AURELIUS (1808–1888; b. Granville, Ohio; active from 1844)

Root studied painting with Thomas Sully and learned the daguerrean art with Robert Cornelius. He was in partnership with David C. Collins, 1844–45; purchased the portrait studio of John Jabez Edwin Mayall in 1846; and opened studios in New York (1849, managed by his brother Samuel) and Washington (1852). Root exhibited at the Institute of American Manufactures from 1844 to 1854, except for 1845. He exhibited his daguerreotype cases in 1852. After his disabling train accident of 1856, he began work on *The Camera and the Pencil*, published in Philadelphia in 1864.

ROOT, SAMUEL (1819–1889; b. Granville, Ohio; active 1849–82)

Learned the daguerrean art from his older brother, Marcus Aurelius, with whom he opened a New York City studio in 1849, the same year he exhibited at the Institute of American Manufactures. He purchased this Franklin and Broadway establishment outright in 1852. Four years later Samuel Root moved to Dubuque, Iowa and continued to work until 1882.

SAXTON, JOSEPH (1799–1873; b. Huntington, Pa.)

Engineer at the United States Mint, made daguerreotypes in October 1839; innovator in photoengraving.

SCHREIBER & SONS (George Francis Schreiber, 1803–1892; b. Germany; active from the late 1840s; firm active into the 1920s)

Portraiture, city views. The elder Schreiber first worked for the Langenheims. By 1857 he was self-employed and the firm soon expanded to include six family members by 1871. They were best known as photographers of animals.

SIMONS, MONTGOMERY P. (1816–1877; active 1845–75)

In partnership with one of the Collinses in 1845. Exhibited daguerreotypes at the Institute of American Manufacture, 1845–48. Simons worked in Richmond, Va., 1851–57. He was the author of manuals, including *Photography in a Nutshell*, Philadelphia, 1858.

TAYLOR, W. CURTIS (active 1863–90)

Portraitist; in partnership with Samuel Broadbent, 1875–79.

WATSON, A. (active ca. 1864)

Photographer for the American Stereoscopic Company, a subsidiary of the Langenheim studio.

WENDEROTH, FREDERICK A. (d. 1884; active from 1860)

Painter in Charleston, S.C. in late 1850s. Worked for Broadbent and Company, ca. 1860; partner in firm Wenderoth, Taylor & Brown, 1866–84. Inventor of the ivorytype.

WILLARD, OLIVER H. (d. 1876; active from 1854)

Portraits, views. Exhibited talbotypes at the Institute of American Manufactures in 1854, ambrotypes and daguerreotypes in 1856.

BIBLIOGRAPHY

PHILADELPHIA HISTORY

Jackson, Joseph. *Encyclopedia of Philadelphia*. Harrisburg: The National Historical Association, 1931.

Philadelphia: Three Centuries of American Art. Philadelphia: Philadelphia Museum of Art, 1976.

Scharf, J. Thomas, and Thompson Westcott. *History of Philadelphia. 1609–1884*. Philadelphia: L. H. Everts, 1884.

Webster, Richard J. *Philadelphia Preserved: Catalog of the Historic American Buildings Survey*. Philadelphia: Temple University Press, 1976.

HISTORY OF PHOTOGRAPHY

Daguerre, [L.-J.-M.]. *An Historical and Descriptive Account of the various Processes of the Daguerréotype and the Diorama*. London: McLean, 1839 (Winter House reprint, 1971).

Newhall, Beaumont. *The Daguerreotype in America*. New York: Dover Publications, 1976. Third revised edition.

——. *The History of Photography from 1839 to the Present Day*. New York: The Museum of Modern Art, 1949.

Szarkowski, John. *The Photographer's Eye*. New York: The Museum of Modern Art, 1966.

Taft, Robert. *Photography and the American Scene: A Social History, 1839–1889*. New York: Macmillan, 1938 (Dover reprint, 1964).

Talbot, William Henry Fox. *The Pencil of Nature*. London: Longman, Brown, Green, & Longmans, 1844–46 (Da Capo reprint, 1969).

Welling, William. *Photography in America: the Formative Years 1839–1900*. New York: Thomas Y. Crowell, 1978.

PHILADELPHIA PHOTOGRAPHY

"Catalogue of the Exhibition of American Manufactures held in the City of Philadelphia, by the Franklin Institute." *Journal of the Franklin Institute*. Philadelphia: 1843–56; 1874.

Catalogue of the Philadelphia Photographic Salon. Philadelphia: [The Pennsylvania Academy of Fine Arts,] 1898–1901.

Catalogue of the Third Annual Exhibition of Photographs. Philadelphia: [The Pennsylvania Academy of Fine Arts, 1889].

Hartmann, Sadakichi. "Elias Goldensky: In the Proletarian Interest." An essay from 1905 in *The Valiant Knights of Daguerre*. Edited by Harry W. Lawton and George Knox. Berkeley: University of California Press, 1978, pp. 215–220.

Jennings, W. N. *Opportunity*. Ms. autobiography [1940] in the Sipley/3M collection at the International Museum of Photography, George Eastman House.

——. "Snapshots from Cloudland." *Journal of the Franklin Institute*. Vol. 218, No. 6, December 1934, pp. 665–684.

McClees, James E. *Elements of Photography*. [Philadelphia: 1855].

Moran, John. "The Relation of Photography to the Fine Arts." *The Philadelphia Photographer*. Vol. 2, No. 15, March 1865, pp. 33–35.

Peale, Rembrandt. "Portraiture." *The Crayon*. Vol. 4, Part 2, February 1857, pp. 44–45.

Philadelphia Photographer, The. Edward L. Wilson, editor. Vols. 1–25 (1864–88).

Root, M. A. *The Camera and the Pencil or the Heliographic Art*. Philadelphia: M. A. Root, 1864.

Sachse, Julius F. "Philadelphia's Share in the Development of Photography." *Journal of the Franklin Institute*. Vol. 135, No. 4, April 1893, pp. 271–287.

Simons, Montgomery P. *Photography in a Nutshell; or, The Experience of An Artist In Photography, on Paper, Glass and Silver*. Philadelphia: King and Baird, 1858.

INDEX

The numbers in italic refer to illustrations; the illustration numbers, not the page numbers, are meant. The abbreviation "n" refers to a note on the respective page.

MAR 20 1981

MAR 2 3 1981

267106 840